HAL LEONARD BANJO METHOD BOOK 1

DELUXE BEGINNER EDITION
For 5-String Banjo

BY MAC ROBERTSON, ROBBIE CLEMENT, AND WILL SCHMID

T0071625

PLAYBACK+
Speed • Pitch • Balance • Loop

To access audio and video, visit:
www.halleonard.com/mylibrary

Enter Code
6993-4113-6612-1188

ISBN 978-1-70517-778-5

Visit Hal Leonard Online at
www.halleonard.com

World headquarters, contact:
Hal Leonard
7777 West Bluemound Road
Milwaukee, WI 53213
Email: info@halleonard.com

In Europe, contact:
Hal Leonard Europe Limited
1 Red Place
London, W1K 6PL
Email: info@halleonardeurope.com

In Australia, contact:
Hal Leonard Australia Pty. Ltd.
4 Lentara Court
Cheltenham, Victoria, 3192 Australia
Email: info@halleonard.com.au

INTRODUCTION

See below to access video and audio!

The *Hal Leonard Banjo Method* teaches the 5-string, bluegrass style. This three-finger style popularized by Earl Scruggs has recently brought the 150-year old American banjo to new prominence. The *Hal Leonard Banjo Method* consists of two books which offer the beginner a *carefully paced approach* to the bluegrass style.

Book 1 Deluxe Beginner Edition features:

- **Audio recordings** for tuning, standard patterns, and songs

- **Video tutorials** and demonstrations by author Mac Robertson

- Easy **chord strums** for the beginner

- Learning **tablature**

- Right-hand **rolls** characteristic of bluegrass

- Classic bluegrass **solos**

- **Licks** such as hammer-ons, slides, and pull-offs

- **Great tunes** like "Cripple Creek" and "Roll in My Sweet Baby's Arms"

Book 2 features:

- More **solos** and standard **licks**

- More great **audio recordings**

- **Melodic-style** banjo

- **Fiddle tunes** such as "Devil's Dream" and "Bill Cheatam"

- Playing **back-up**

- Use of the **capo** and more **music theory**

ABOUT THE AUDIO AND VIDEO ▶ VIDEO 2

The audio tracks and video tutorials are marked and numbered throughout this book. You can access them online by visiting *www.halleonard.com/mylibrary* and entering the code printed on page 1 of this book. From here you can stream or download the files at your convenience!

BANJO PARTS ▶ VIDEO 3

Strings
Head
Bridge
Tailpiece
5th-String Peg
Sliding 5th-String Capo
Fingerboard
1st Fret
2nd Fret
Peghead (Headstock)
Nut
Tuning Pegs (Keys)
Neck
Position Markers (Inlays)
Heel
Brackets
Tension Hoop
Rim
Resonator

TUNING

When you are tuning your banjo, you will adjust the **pitch** (highness or lowness) of each string by turning the corresponding tuning key. Tightening a string raises the pitch; loosening a string lowers the pitch.

The strings are numbered 1 through 5. The fifth string is the shortest on the banjo.

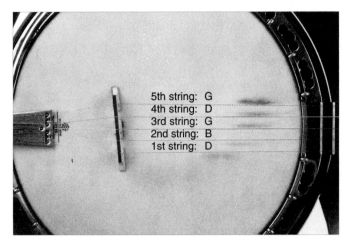

5th string: G
4th string: D
3rd string: G
2nd string: B
1st string: D

TUNING TO THE RECORDING

You will hear each string played three times. Turn the tuning key for each string until the sound of the string matches the sound on the recording. If the two sounds grow farther apart, you are turning the key in the wrong direction. If they sound closer together, you are turning the key in the right direction.

Let's Begin

TRACK 2

The first tuning note you'll hear is for the fourth string D

TRACK 3

The next tuning note is for string three (G)

TRACK 4

String two (B)

TRACK 5

String one (D)

TRACK 6

String five (G)

This is known as *Open G tuning* and will be used throughout this book.

TUNING TO A PIANO OR ELECTRONIC TUNER

When not using the recording you can tune your banjo to a piano, an electronic tuner, or itself. An electronic tuner gives the player a visual indication when each string is in tune. Banjo tuning requires a chromatic twelve-pitch tuner rather than a tuner intended specifically for guitar with six pitches.

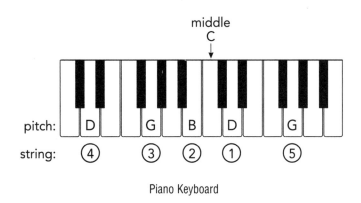

Piano Keyboard

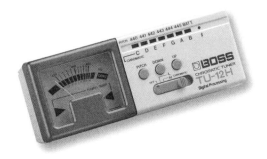

Electronic Tuner

TUNING A BANJO TO ITSELF

To tune a banjo to itself follow these steps:

Step 1. Begin by tuning the open fourth string to D. (An open string is a string not being pressed down by a finger).

It is highly recommended that the fourth string be matched to a starting pitch. Otherwise, a string tuned too high beyond its intended pitch may break.

Step 2. Press the fourth string at the *fifth* fret (see illustration). This is the pitch G to which you tune your open third string. Continue plucking the third string as you adjust the third tuning key. When the two sounds match, you are in tune.

Step 3. Press the third string at the *fourth* fret, and tune the open second string to it. Follow the same procedure that you did on the third and fourth strings.

Step 4. Press the second string at the *third* fret and tune the open first string to it.

Step 5. Finally, press the first string at the *fifth* fret and tune the open fifth string to it.

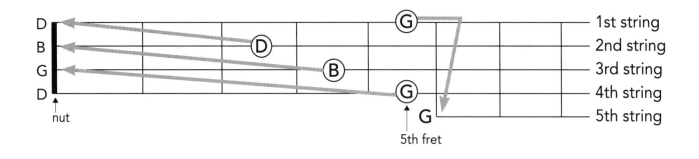

HOW TO HOLD YOUR BANJO ▶ VIDEO 5

Place the banjo between your legs, and use the right arm to hold it against your body. The neck of the banjo should point to the left at about a 45 degree angle from the floor.

Whether you are sitting or standing, you will need a strap to hold your banjo. Attach the strap below the neck and on the bracket just above the tailpiece. The most common way of wearing a strap is over the left shoulder and under the right arm.

LEFT-HAND POSITION

- Place your thumb on the backside of the banjo neck as shown in the photo.

- Allow your hand to curve around the neck and arch your fingers over the strings.

- Don't let the palm of your hand touch the neck of the banjo. Keep your wrist straight.

PLAYING CHORDS

LET'S PLAY & SING

In this section of the book you'll be playing more than one note or string at the same time. This sound is called a **chord**. The first chords that you will learn (G, D7, C, G7) are used strictly to accompany the melody which you'll sing.

Notice the slash marks above the lyrics of the song "Frère Jacques" on this page. Each slash mark or chord letter indicates *one* strum. A basic strum on the banjo is the thumb strum. The thumb of the right hand is brushed down across the strings.

THE G CHORD ▶ VIDEO 6

The accompanying chord diagram uses open circles to indicate open strings. No left-hand fingers are touching these strings.

When you strum across the strings with all strings "open," you are sounding the G chord. Practice strumming the G chord with a steady beat. You are now ready to play the accompaniment to "Frère Jacques."

At the beginning of each song you'll see the words, "Starting Singing Pitch:" followed by the name of the note on which you begin singing. Pluck this note and hum the pitch before you start.

Practice each song until you can play it well, then go on to the next song. Keep a steady strum as you sing.

FRÈRE JACQUES

TRACK 7

Starting Singing Pitch: Open third string (G)

G   /   /   /   /   /   /   /
Are   you   sleep - ing,   are   you   sleep - ing,

/   /   /   /   /   /   /   /
Broth - er   John,   broth - er   John?

/   /   /   /   /   /   /   /
Morn - ing bells are ring - ing,   morn - ing bells are ring - ing.

/   /   /   /   /   /   /   /
Ding,   dong,   ding.   ding,   dong,   ding.

LEFT-HAND FINGER NUMBERS

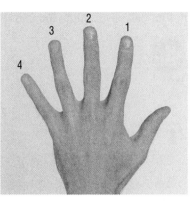

You have played a song that used only an open-string G chord. To play other chords, you will need to press the strings at the correct frets with your left-hand fingers. The left-hand fingers are numbered from the index finger (1) to the little finger (4).

THE D7 CHORD ▶ VIDEO 7

Study the diagram for the D7 chord. Arch your fingers and touch only the tips of fingers one and two in the positions indicated. Strum the D7 chord.

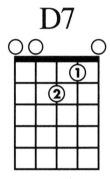

D7   /   /   /   /   /   /   /

Now try the following exercise which uses both the G chord and the D7 chord. When you are playing the open G chord, keep your fingers in position over the strings. This will help you change from one chord to the next quickly.

Keep the beat steady. Remember to strum once for each letter or slash mark.

D7   /   /   /   G   /   /   /   D7   /   /   /   G   /   /   /

BEATS

Music is arranged into groups of **beats** or **pulses**. At the beginning of each song you'll see a number. This number tells you how many beats are in a group. Most of the songs you'll be playing will have two, three, or four beats in a group, and you should strum once for each beat. "Rock-A-My Soul" has slash marks in the first verse to help you get started.

ROCK-A-MY SOUL

Starting Singing Pitch: Open second string (B)

TRACK 8

4

G   /   /   /   /   /   /   /
1. Rock-a-my   soul   in the bos-om of   A-bra-ham,

D7   /   /   /   /   /   /   /
Rock-a-my   soul   in the bos-om of   A-bra-ham,

G   /   /   /   /   /   /   /
Rock-a-my   soul   in the bos-om of   A-bra-ham,

D7   /   /   /   G   /   /
Oh,   rock-a-my   soul!

G
2. So high, I can't get over it.

D7
So low, I can't get under it.

G
So wide, I can't get 'round it.

D7   G
Oh, rock-a-my soul!

9

In the following songs, the chord slashes will be shown only above the first two lines.

HUSH LITTLE BABY

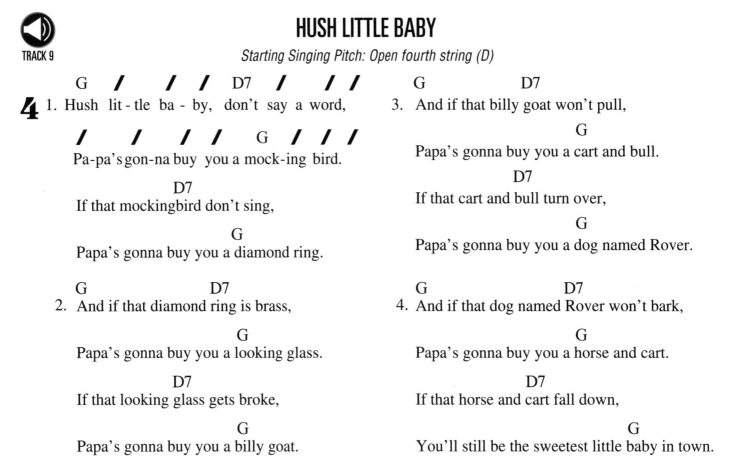

TRACK 9

Starting Singing Pitch: Open fourth string (D)

G / / / **D7** / / /
4 1. Hush lit‑tle ba‑by, don't say a word,

/ / / / **G** / / /
Pa‑pa's gon‑na buy you a mock‑ing bird.

D7
If that mockingbird don't sing,

G
Papa's gonna buy you a diamond ring.

G **D7**
2. And if that diamond ring is brass,

G
Papa's gonna buy you a looking glass.

D7
If that looking glass gets broke,

G
Papa's gonna buy you a billy goat.

G **D7**
3. And if that billy goat won't pull,

G
Papa's gonna buy you a cart and bull.

D7
If that cart and bull turn over,

G
Papa's gonna buy you a dog named Rover.

G **D7**
4. And if that dog named Rover won't bark,

G
Papa's gonna buy you a horse and cart.

D7
If that horse and cart fall down,

G
You'll still be the sweetest little baby in town.

The song "Clementine" is the first song you have with groups of three beats. Strum once for each beat.

CLEMENTINE

TRACK 10

Starting Singing Pitch: Open third string (G)

G / / / / / / / **D7** /
3 1. In a cav‑ern, in a can‑yon, ex‑ca‑vat‑ing for a mine,

/ / / / **G** / / **D7** / / **G** /
Lived a min‑er, for‑ty‑nin‑er, and his daugh‑ter Clem‑en‑tine.

G **D7**
CHORUS: Oh my darling, oh my darling, oh my darling Clementine.

G **D7** **G**
You are lost and gone forever, dreadful sorry, Clementine.

G **D7**
2. Drove she ducklings to the water, every morning just at nine,

G **D7** **G**
Stubbed her toe against a splinter, fell into the foaming brine. *CHORUS*

G **D7**
3. Ruby lips above the water, blowing bubbles soft and fine,

G **D7** **G**
But alas, I was no swimmer, so I lost my Clementine. *CHORUS*

THE C CHORD 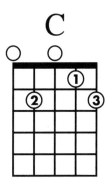 VIDEO 8

Study the diagram for the finger position of the C chord.

Practice playing the C and G chords in the following exercises.

Remember to keep the fingers in position over the strings when you are playing the open G chord.

4 C / / / G / / / C / / / G / / /

3 C / / G / / C / / G / /

TRACK 11

DOWN IN THE VALLEY

Starting Singing Pitch: Open third string (G)

C / / / / / / / / / G / /

3 1. Down in the val - ley, val-ley so low;

                                                          C

Hang your head over, hear the wind blow.

                                                      G

Hear the wind blow, dear, hear the wind blow;

                                                      C

Hang your head over, hear the wind blow.

       C   G

2. Roses love sunshine, violets love dew,

                                    C

Angels in heaven know I love you.

                                          G

Know I love you, dear, know I love you,

                                    C

Angels in heaven know I love you.

       C   G

3. Build me a castle, forty feet high,

                                    C

So I may see him as he rides by.

                                          G

As he rides by, dear, as he rides by,

                                    C

So I may see him as he rides by.

Now practice all three chords in "Oh, Susanna" and "Do Lord."

OH, SUSANNA

Starting Singing Pitch: Open third string (G)

G / / / / / / / / / / / **D7** / /
4 1. Oh, I come from Al - a - bam - a with a ban - jo on my knee.

/ **G** / / / / / / / / **D7** / **G** / /
I'm go-in' to Lou' - si - an - a, my true love for to see.

                                                 D7
It rained all night the day I left, the weather it was dry.

   G   **D7**   **G**
The sun so hot, I froze myself. Susanna, don't you cry.

             C   **G**   **D7**
CHORUS: Oh, Susanna, now don't you cry for me,

               G   **D7**   **G**
For I come from Alabama with a banjo on my knee.

 G   **D7**
2. I had a dream the other night when everything was still.

   G   **D7**   **G**
I thought I saw Susanna a-comin' down the hill.

                                           D7
The buckwheat cake was in her mouth, the tear was in her eye.

   G   **D7**   **G**
Says I, "I'm comin' from the South," Susanna, don't you cry. *CHORUS*

DO LORD

Starting Singing Pitch: Open fourth string (D)

G / / / / / / / / / / / / / / /
4 *CHORUS:* Do Lord, oh, do Lord, oh, do re-mem-ber me.

C / / / / / / / / / / / / **G** / / /
Do Lord, oh, do Lord, oh, do re-mem-ber me.

Do Lord, oh, do Lord, oh, do remember me.

               D7   **G**
Look away beyond the blue.

 G
1. I got a home in glory land that outshines the sun.
 C   **G**
I got a home in glory land that outshines the sun.

I got a home in glory land that outshines the sun.
          D7   **G**
Look away beyond the blue. *CHORUS*

2. When my blood runs chilly and cold, I got to go.
When my blood runs chilly and cold, I got to go.
When my blood runs chilly and cold, I got to go.
Look away beyond the blue. *CHORUS*

THE G7 CHORD 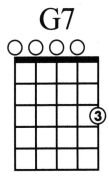 ▶ VIDEO 9

G7

Another easy chord on banjo is the G7 chord. Place the third finger at the third fret of the first string as shown in the diagram. Then play the next two songs which use the G7 chord.

TRACK 14

HE'S GOT THE WHOLE WORLD IN HIS HANDS

Starting Singing Pitch: Open third string (G)

CHORUS:

4 C / / / / / /
He's got the whole wor - ld in His hands,
/ G7 / / / / /
He's got the whole wide wor - ld in His hands,
C
He's got the whole world in His hands,
G7   C
He's got the whole world in His hands.

C
1. He's got the little bitty baby in His hands,
G7
He's got the little bitty baby in His hands,
C
He's got the little bitty baby in His hands,
G7   C
He's got the whole world in His hands.
CHORUS

C
2. He's got you and me, brother, in His hands,
G7
He's got you and me, brother, in His hands,
C
He's got you and me, brother, in His hands,
G7   C
He's got the whole world in His hands.
CHORUS

C
3. He's got you and me, sister, in His hands,
G7
He's got you and me, sister, in His hands,
C
He's got you and me, sister, in His hands,
G7   C
He's got the whole world in His hands.
CHORUS

THIS OLD MAN

Starting Singing Pitch: Open third string (G)

TRACK 15

4 C / / / / / /
1. This old man, he played one,
G7 / / / / / /
He played knick-knack on my thumb,
C
With a knick-knack paddy whack, give a dog a bone,
G7   C
This old man came rolling home.

C
2. This old man, he played two,
G7
He played knick-knack on my shoe,
C
With a knick-knack paddy whack, give a dog a bone,
G7   C
This old man came rolling home.

3. three — knee

4. four — door

5. five — hive

6. six — sticks

7. seven — heaven

8. eight — gate

9. nine — spine

10. ten — hen

13

VIDEO 10

The next two songs are grouped in two beats. Play one strum for each beat as you sing the melody. In "She'll Be Comin' 'Round the Mountain" you don't start to strum until after the first two words are sung.

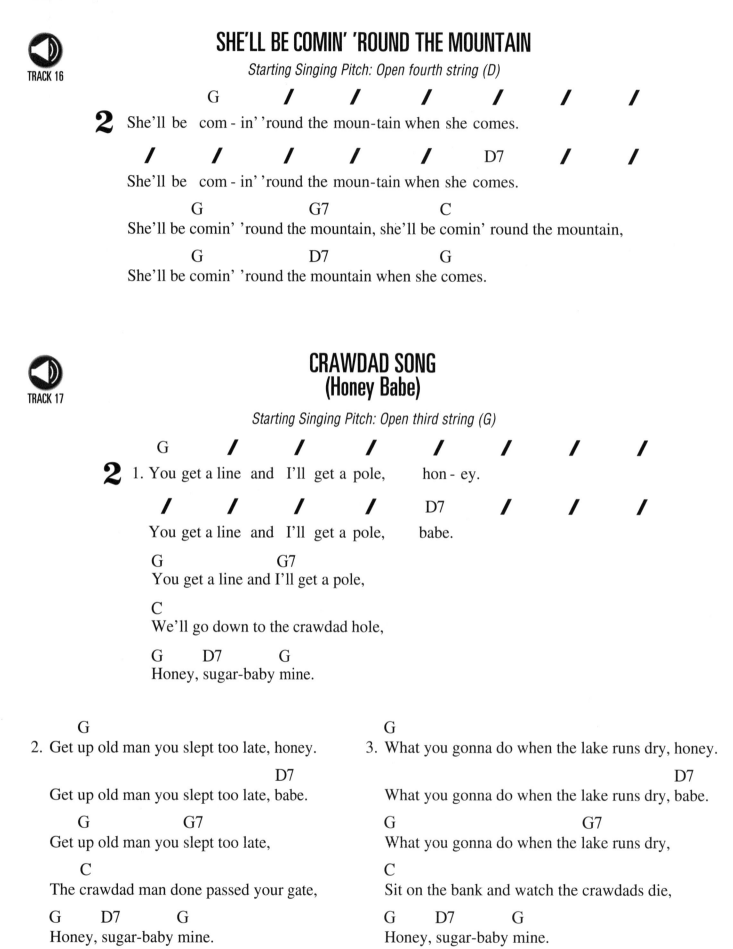

TRACK 16

SHE'LL BE COMIN' 'ROUND THE MOUNTAIN

Starting Singing Pitch: Open fourth string (D)

2 G   /   /   /   /   /   /
She'll be com-in' 'round the moun-tain when she comes.

/   /   /   /   /   D7   /   /
She'll be com-in' 'round the moun-tain when she comes.

G   G7   C
She'll be comin' 'round the mountain, she'll be comin' round the mountain,

G   D7   G
She'll be comin' 'round the mountain when she comes.

TRACK 17

CRAWDAD SONG
(Honey Babe)

Starting Singing Pitch: Open third string (G)

2 G   /   /   /   /   /   /
1. You get a line and I'll get a pole,   hon-ey.

/   /   /   /   D7   /   /   /
You get a line and I'll get a pole,   babe.

G   G7
You get a line and I'll get a pole,

C
We'll go down to the crawdad hole,

G   D7   G
Honey, sugar-baby mine.

G
2. Get up old man you slept too late, honey.

         D7
Get up old man you slept too late, babe.

G   G7
Get up old man you slept too late,

C
The crawdad man done passed your gate,

G   D7   G
Honey, sugar-baby mine.

G
3. What you gonna do when the lake runs dry, honey.

         D7
What you gonna do when the lake runs dry, babe.

G   G7
What you gonna do when the lake runs dry,

C
Sit on the bank and watch the crawdads die,

G   D7   G
Honey, sugar-baby mine.

TABLATURE

VIDEO 11

Tablature (tab) is a means of notating left-hand finger positions by giving the number of the fret where the finger belongs. The numbers are placed on a series of lines that represent the strings of the banjo, starting with the fifth string at the bottom of the diagram.

1st string: D
2nd string: B
3rd string: G
4th string: D
5th string: G

If there is a "0" on a line, play the string open. In the illustration below the open third string should be plucked.

This diagram indicates that the second string is pressed at the first fret.

A strum across an open G chord should look like this:

TIME SIGNATURES 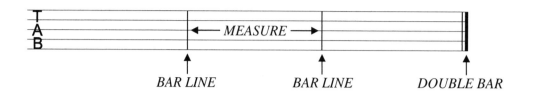 VIDEO 12

When you began strumming chords, you played a chord whenever there was a chord letter or a diagonal slash. This was a pulse or beat.

You have already learned that music is arranged by groups of two, three, or four beats. One of these groups is called a **measure** and is indicated in tablature with **bar lines**. A **double bar** line is used to end a piece of music.

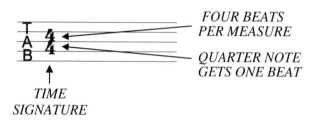

At the beginning of each song there will be two numbers called a **time signature**. The top number will tell you how many beats are in one measure. The bottom number tells you what kind of note receives one beat.

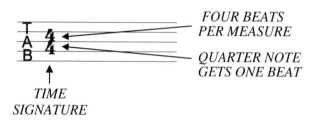

QUARTER NOTES AND RESTS

The **quarter note** gets one beat when the number 4 is at the bottom of a time signature. The quarter note is indicated by a vertical line below the tab number. Below are several different quarter notes.

QUARTER
NOTES
(one beat each)

Another kind of sign used in tab is the **rest**. Rests indicate silence or no sound. When a rest replaces a quarter note (one beat), it is called a **quarter rest**. Both the quarter note and the quarter rest get one beat in 4/4 time.

QUARTER
RESTS
(one beat each)

VIDEO 13

Count carefully as you practice the following exercise. Remember that a quarter note gets one beat. Use your right-hand thumb to pluck the notes. All of the following notes are played on the open first string.

TRACK 18

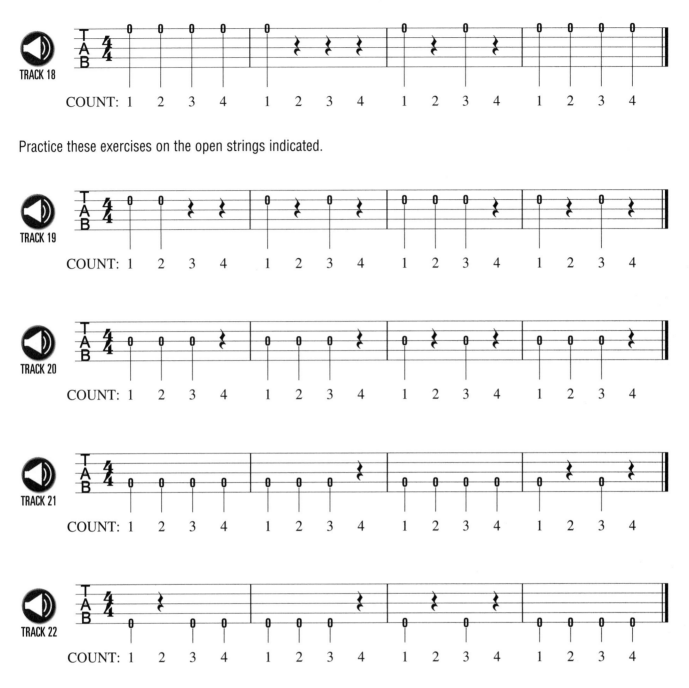

Practice these exercises on the open strings indicated.

TRACK 19

TRACK 20

TRACK 21

TRACK 22

MORE RESTS

Sometimes rests last longer than one beat. A two-beat rest is called a **half rest** and sits *above* the middle line. A four-beat rest is called a **whole rest** and hangs *below* the fourth line.

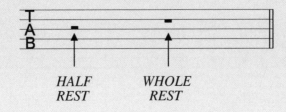

HALF REST   *WHOLE REST*

PLAYING NOTES

NOTES ON THE THIRD STRING: G & A

Now it's time to learn some notes. The note G is simply the open third string. When you play the note A, press your left-hand 2nd finger down on the third string, just behind the 2nd fret, and pluck the string with your right-hand thumb. Strive for a clean, clear sound.

As you are playing the following exercise, look ahead to the next note, and get your fingers ready. Keep your fingers just above the strings until you are ready to play the note. Always count and keep the beat steady. Practice the exercise until you can play it well.

NOTES ON THE SECOND STRING: B & C

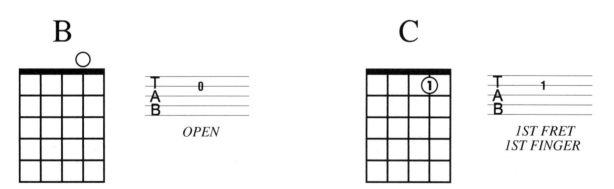

Practice this exercise using the new notes B and C. Count out loud as you play, and give each note or rest its full value. Keep the beat steady.

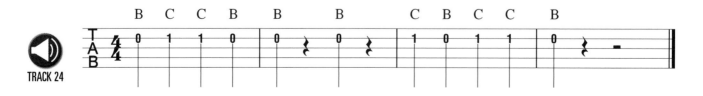

MOVING FROM STRING TO STRING

In the following exercises, you will be moving from string to string to play the four notes that you already know. As you are playing one note, look ahead to the next, and get your fingers ready. Notice that the first exercise continues to the second line. We read music like we read words—from left to right.

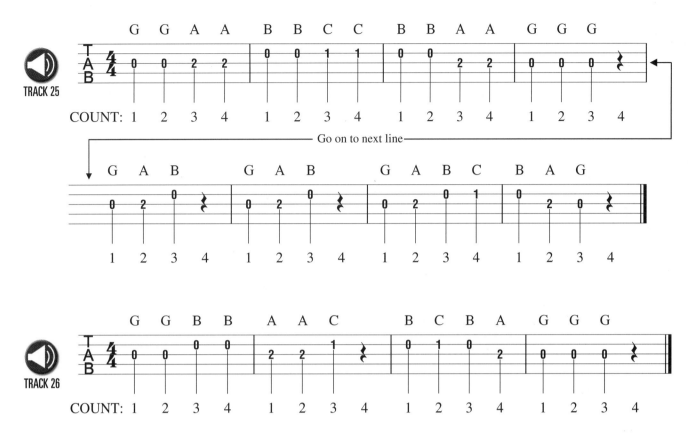

TRACK 25

Go on to next line

TRACK 26

NOTES ON THE FIRST STRING: D

D

Practice the following exercises that include notes from the first three strings. Watch the numbers and the strings carefully. Practice slowly and steadily. Use your right-hand thumb to play these exercises.

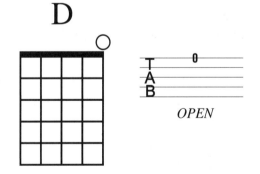

OPEN

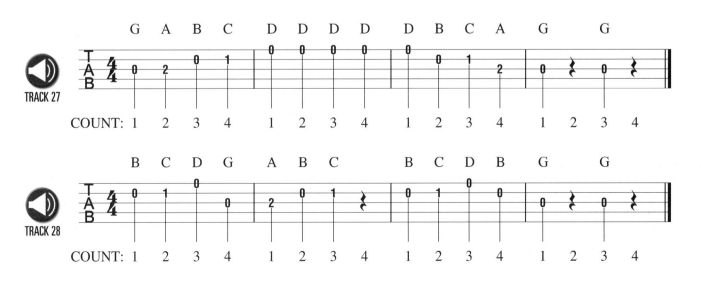

TRACK 27

TRACK 28

19

LEARNING RHYTHM

2/4 TIME  VIDEO 14

In this time signature, the top number tells you there are two beats per measure and a quarter note gets one beat.

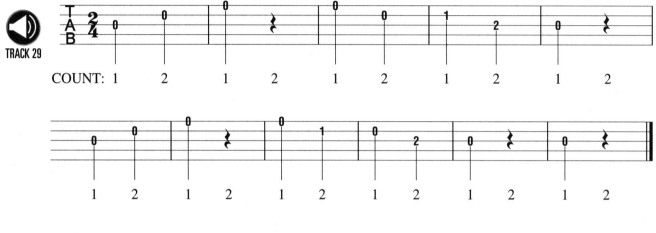

TWO BEATS
PER MEASURE

QUARTER NOTE
GETS ONE BEAT

Practice the new time signature in the following exercise.

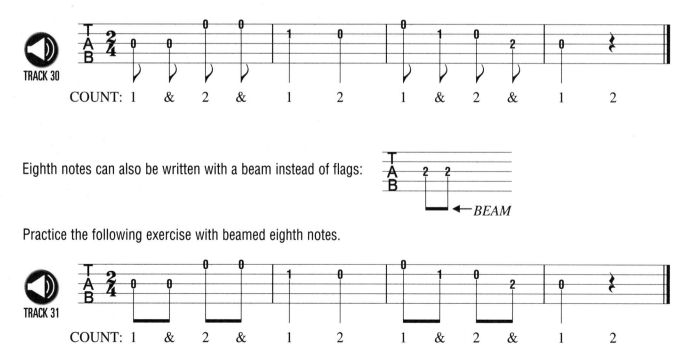

TRACK 29

COUNT: 1   2   1   2   1   2   1   2   1   2

1   2   1   2   1   2   1   2   1   2   1   2

EIGHT NOTES

A note that receives a half beat is called an **eighth note**.
Single eighth notes are written like quarter notes with a flag:

← *FLAG*

Since quarter notes receive one beat, there are two eighth notes per beat. An easy way to count eighth notes is "1 & 2 &." Tap your foot on the beat. Practice playing quarter notes and eighth notes in the following example.

TRACK 30

COUNT: 1   &   2   &   1   2   1   &   2   &   1   2

Eighth notes can also be written with a beam instead of flags:

← *BEAM*

Practice the following exercise with beamed eighth notes.

TRACK 31

COUNT: 1   &   2   &   1   2   1   &   2   &   1   2

20

Now play a familiar tune written in tablature. Count carefully and practice slowly to learn the **rhythm** (combination of time values) and the notes. Then sing the words as you strum the chords indicated above the tab. Remember to play one chord strum on each beat, changing chords as new letters are given.

MERRILY WE ROLL ALONG

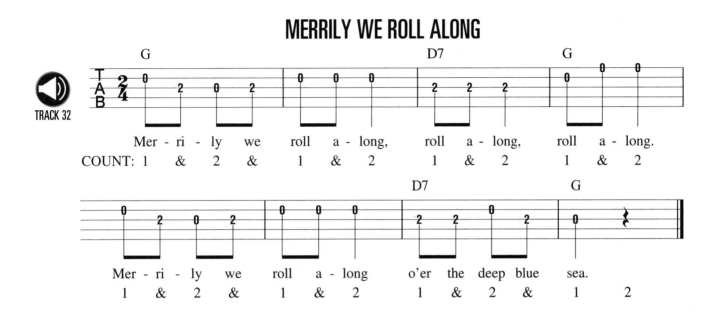

TRACK 32

HALF NOTES

Notes that get two beats are called **half notes**. Half notes are indicated by a circle around the fret number. Half notes are twice as long as quarter notes and should be allowed to ring for their full value.

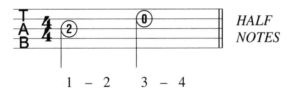

HALF NOTES

VIDEO 15

The song "Aunt Rhody" uses all three types of notes that you now know. Practice counting aloud as you play the melody. Let the final half note ring for two full beats.

AUNT RHODY

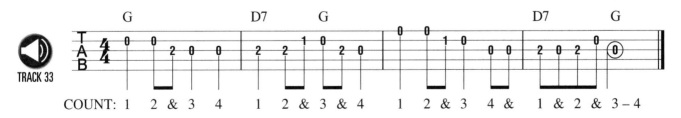

TRACK 33

21

RIGHT-HAND POSITION ▶ VIDEO 16

Bluegrass banjo playing is known for its bright tone. Fingerpicks help create this characteristic sound. On the index and middle fingers you should wear metal picks. A plastic pick is worn on the thumb. The curve of the fingerpick follows the curve of the finger. Study the photos for the correct position of the picks.

The metal picks may be adjusted with a pliers. The plastic pick may be softened by immersing it in boiling water with the pliers and then shaping it to fit tightly around your thumb.

Let your right hand curl loosely over the strings near the bridge. Rest your third and fourth fingers lightly on the banjo head to steady your hand. Keep the wrist arched and fingers relaxed so they can function freely and independently.

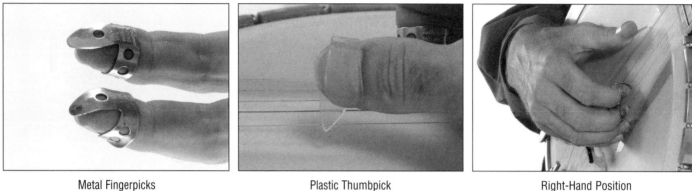

Metal Fingerpicks   Plastic Thumbpick   Right-Hand Position

RULES FOR RIGHT-HAND FINGERPICKING

- The thumb (t) strikes downward to play notes on strings 3, 4, and 5.

- The index finger (i) picks upward to play notes on string 2.

- The middle finger (m) picks upward to play notes on string 1.

Try the exercise below while paying careful attention to the right-hand thumb and finger indications (t, i, and m) below each note.

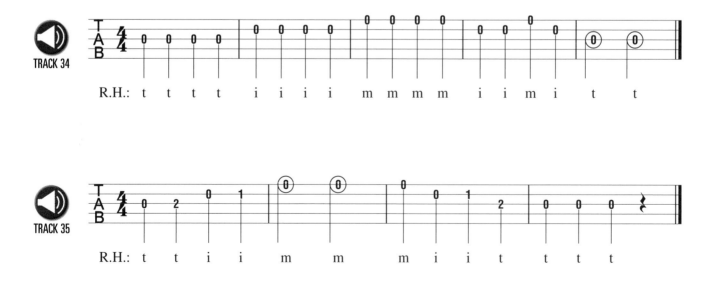

MORE FIRST-STRING NOTES: E & F

You have learned that the note D is played on the open first string. Look at the diagrams below for the correct finger positions for E and F. Pluck all notes on the first string with the middle finger.

Play this exercise to become familiar with the new notes. Use only the middle finger (m) of the right hand to pick the notes.

VIDEO 17

TRACK 36

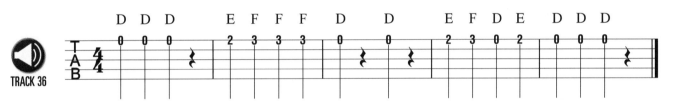

Now practice using the new notes in "Old Joe Clark." Watch the right-hand fingerings.

OLD JOE CLARK

TRACK 37

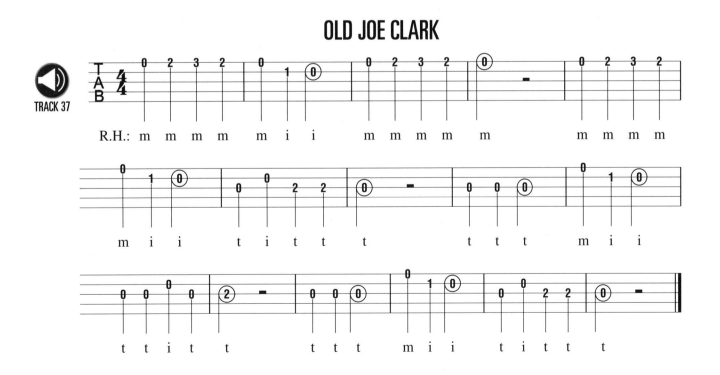

THE F CHORD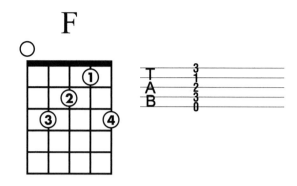

VIDEO 18

Study the diagram for the finger position of the F chord.

F

Practice singing and strumming "Old Joe Clark" which uses the new F chord. Be sure you can change chords smoothly and keep the beat steady.

OLD JOE CLARK

TRACK 38

4/4
G / / / / / / / / / / F / / /
1. Old   Joe   Clark,   the   preach-er's   son,   preached   all   o-ver   the   plain,

G / / / / / / / / / D7 / G / / /
The   on - ly   text   he   ev - er   knew   was "high,   low   jack, and   the   game."

                      G   F
          CHORUS: Fare thee well old Joe Clark, fare thee well I say.

                      G   D7   G
          Fare thee well old Joe Clark, I'm a-goin' away.

G   F
2. Won't go down to old Joe's house, tell you the reason why,

G   D7   G
Can't get through his garden patch, for tearin' down his rye. *CHORUS*

G   F
3. Wish I was in Arkansas, sittin' on a rail,

G   D7   G
Jug of moonshine under my arm, possum by the tail. *CHORUS*

G   F
4. Old Joe Clark had a yellow cat, would neither sing nor pray,

G   D7 G
Stuck her head in a buttermilk jar, and washed her sins away. *CHORUS*

G   F
5. Wish I was in Bowling Green, sittin' in the sun,

G   D7   G
Never saw a pretty little girl, I couldn't love her some. *CHORUS*

For extra practice, ask a friend to play either chords or melody while you play the other, or record one part and play along with the recording.

RIGHT-HAND ROLLS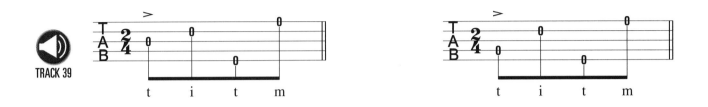

Bluegrass banjo playing is characterized by a continuous series of notes picked by the right hand. These notes may be divided into basic patterns called **rolls**.

Although the rolls may sound difficult, they are easy to learn if you separate them into small sections and practice them slowly and carefully. Concentrate on steady, solid picking and the speed will develop later.

Practice the following four-note rolls until you can play them smoothly and steadily. The symbol (>) is an **accent** mark and indicates that the note below it should be played louder than the others.

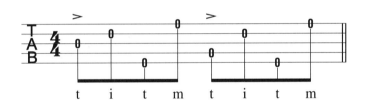

TRACK 39

THE ALTERNATING THUMB ROLL VIDEO 20

An **alternating thumb roll** always uses the pattern "titm," no matter which notes are played. Combining the two four-note patterns you have learned produces the following common alternating thumb roll. Note that the first thumb stroke changes back and forth between the third and fourth strings.

Now practice the alternating thumb roll until you can play it easily. Gradually speed up, keeping the notes even as you play.

REPEAT SIGNS & ENDINGS

The double bar with two dots 𝄇 tells you to **repeat** the section that you have just played. There will usually be a repeat sign at the beginning of a section to be repeated. If there is no repeat sign, return to the beginning of the song.

The numbered brackets ⌐1.⌐ and ⌐2.⌐ are called the **first** and **second endings**. The rules for using these endings are:

- Play the first section of music through the first ending.

- At the repeat sign 𝄇 return to the beginning of the section.

- Skip over the first ending on the repeat, and go directly to the second ending.

25

We will now play the alternating thumb roll as accompaniment to three familiar songs, "Rock-A-My Soul," "Aunt Rhody," and "Hush Little Baby." Both the melody (top tab) and the picking pattern (bottom tab) are shown. First practice the melody on the banjo, then sing it and strum the chords. When you can do this easily, try the alternating thumb roll.

Practice the following exercise.

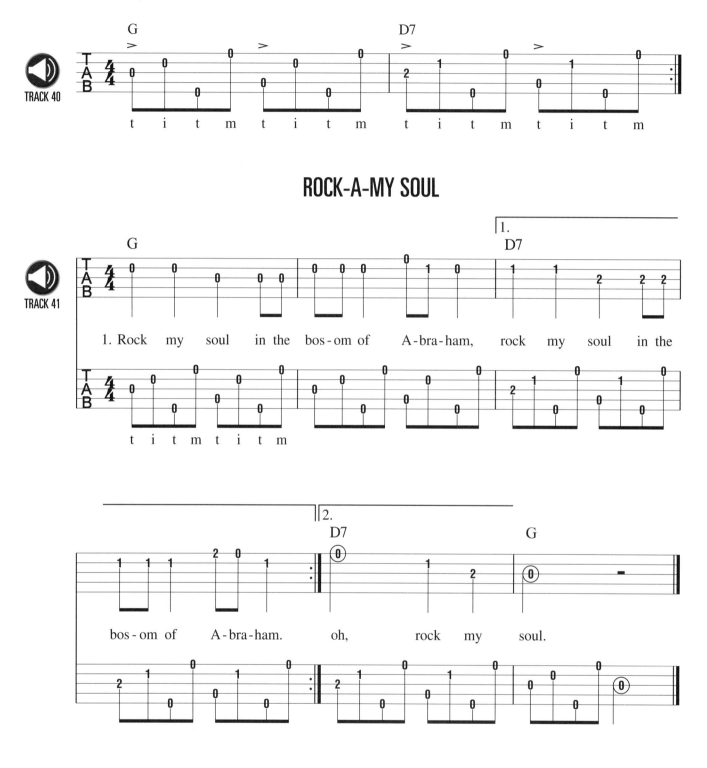

ROCK-A-MY SOUL

1. Rock my soul in the bos-om of A-bra-ham, rock my soul in the

bos-om of A-bra-ham. oh, rock my soul.

        G   D7
2. So high, you can't get over it. So low, you can't get under it.

        G   D7   G
So wide, you can't get 'round it. Oh, rock my soul.

AUNT RHODY

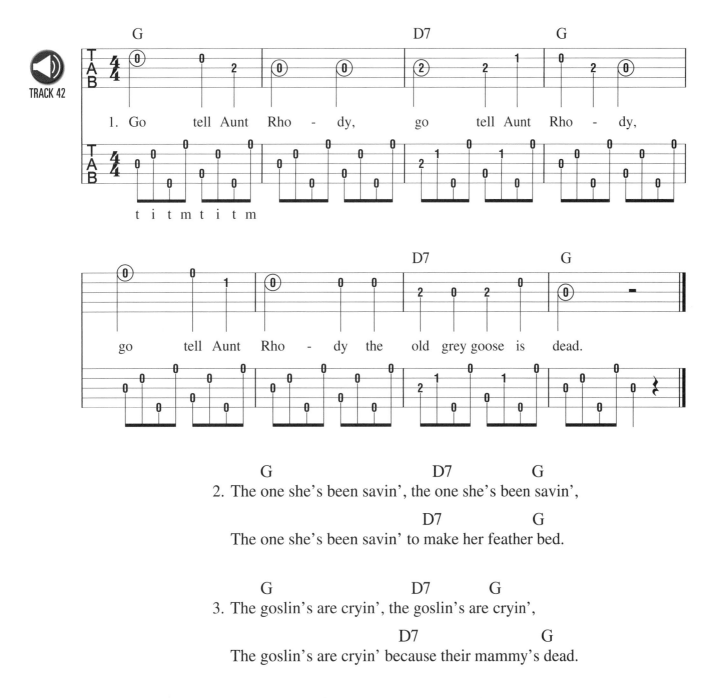

TRACK 42

1. Go tell Aunt Rho - dy, go tell Aunt Rho - dy,

t i t m t i t m

go tell Aunt Rho - dy the old grey goose is dead.

        G   D7   G

2. The one she's been savin', the one she's been savin',

                            D7   G

The one she's been savin' to make her feather bed.

        G   D7   G

3. The goslin's are cryin', the goslin's are cryin',

                            D7   G

The goslin's are cryin' because their mammy's dead.

BOUNCY RHYTHM FEEL

VIDEO 21

TRACK 43 TRACK 44
straight   bouncy

The recording presents two versions of the alternating thumb roll. In the first example (Track 43) the notes are played exactly as notated with each note receiving the same time value. In the second example (Track 44) the roll sounds "bouncy" because the rhythm has been altered slightly. This bouncy rhythm is an important part of "bluegrass sound."

To make the bouncy sound, the first eighth note of each pair is lengthened, and as a result the second eighth note is shortened. You'll sometimes hear this called **swing** or **shuffle feel**.

Listen to the recording, then try both ways of playing the alternating roll with "Rock-A-My Soul," "Aunt Rhody," and "Hush Little Baby."

Although all the rolls in this book are written in equal eighth notes, you should practice them with and without the bounce.

HUSH LITTLE BABY

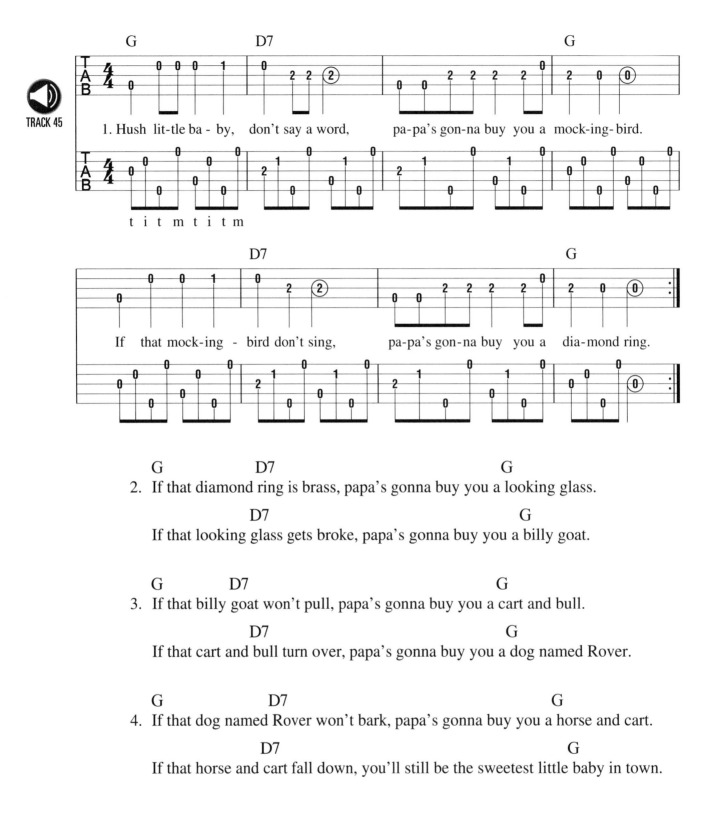

TRACK 45

1. Hush lit-tle ba - by,   don't say a word,   pa-pa's gon-na buy you a mock-ing-bird.

t i t m t i t m

If that mock-ing - bird don't sing,   pa-pa's gon-na buy you a dia-mond ring.

G   D7   G
2. If that diamond ring is brass, papa's gonna buy you a looking glass.
         D7   G
   If that looking glass gets broke, papa's gonna buy you a billy goat.

G   D7   G
3. If that billy goat won't pull, papa's gonna buy you a cart and bull.
         D7   G
   If that cart and bull turn over, papa's gonna buy you a dog named Rover.

G   D7   G
4. If that dog named Rover won't bark, papa's gonna buy you a horse and cart.
         D7   G
   If that horse and cart fall down, you'll still be the sweetest little baby in town.

FOURTH-STRING NOTES: D, E & F

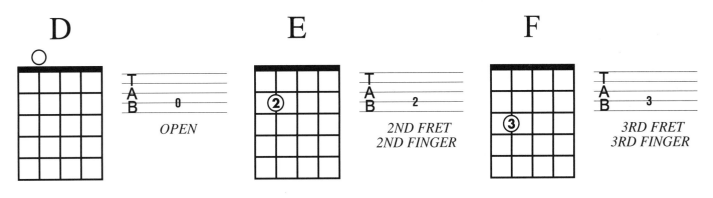

D	E	F
OPEN	2ND FRET 2ND FINGER	3RD FRET 3RD FINGER

Practice the following exercises with these new notes. Play all notes on the fourth string with your right-hand thumb.

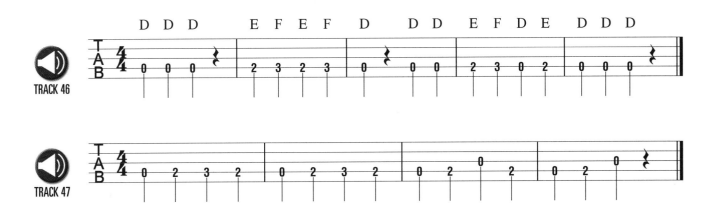

TRACK 46

TRACK 47

PICKUP NOTES

Music doesn't always begin on beat one. When you begin after beat one, the notes before the first full measure are called **pickup notes**. Here are several examples of pickup notes. Count the missing beats out loud before you begin playing.

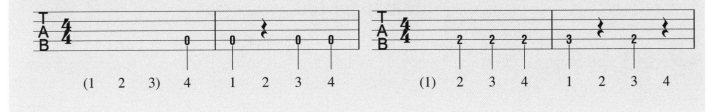

This melody starts with a pickup note.

MINOR MELODY

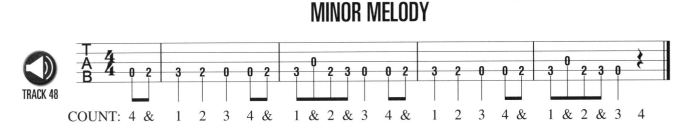

TRACK 48

HALF & WHOLE STEPS

The distance between music tones is measured by **half steps** and **whole steps**. On your banjo the distance between one fret and the next fret is one half step. The distance from one fret to the second fret in either direction is called a whole step.

A **sharp** (♯) raises a note by one half step. Since F is played on the fourth string, third fret, F sharp is played on the fourth string, fourth fret.

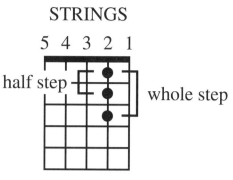

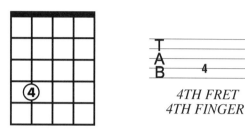

Play these exercises to become familiar with F sharp.

 TRACK 49

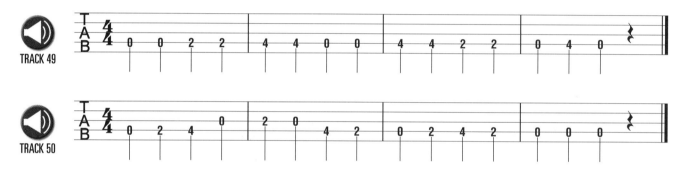 **TRACK 50**

Now practice some familiar songs that have F sharp in them.

SKIP TO MY LOU

TRACK 51

BLUE TAIL FLY

TRACK 52

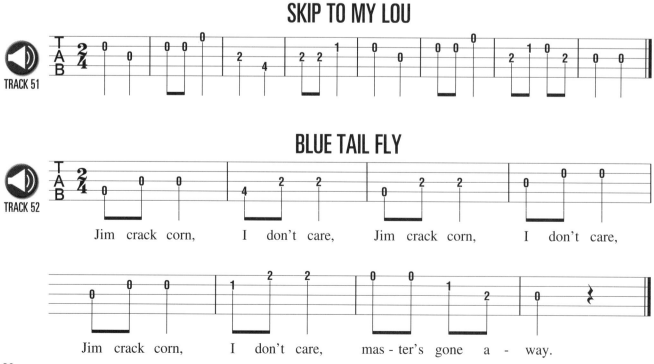

Jim crack corn,   I don't care,   Jim crack corn,   I don't care,

Jim crack corn,   I don't care,   mas - ter's gone a - way.

THE FIFTH STRING: G

The fifth string is the highest-sounding open string on a banjo, and the note G is played on the open string.

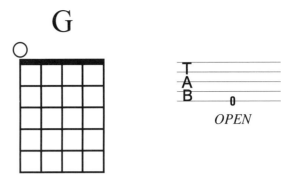

Try out the fifth-string G in this exercise.

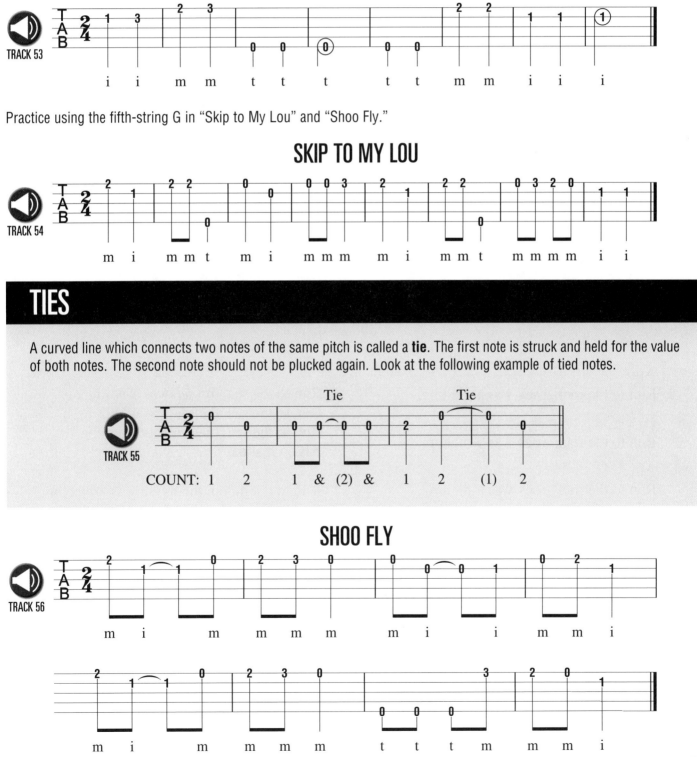

Practice using the fifth-string G in "Skip to My Lou" and "Shoo Fly."

SKIP TO MY LOU

TIES

A curved line which connects two notes of the same pitch is called a **tie**. The first note is struck and held for the value of both notes. The second note should not be plucked again. Look at the following example of tied notes.

SHOO FLY

THE Am CHORD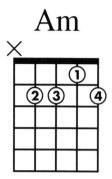

VIDEO 22

The small "m" after the "A" tells you this is a minor chord. Notice that the fourth finger is placed at the second fret of the first string, and the short fifth string is not played.

Am

First practice playing the melody to "Oh, Sinner Man." Watch for the high G in measures 2 and 6. When you know the melody well, strum the chords as accompaniment to singing.

OH, SINNER MAN

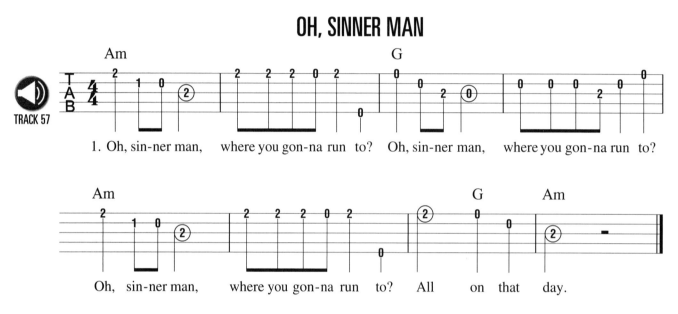

TRACK 57

1. Oh, sin-ner man, where you gon-na run to? Oh, sin-ner man, where you gon-na run to?

Oh, sin-ner man, where you gon-na run to? All on that day.

Am
2. Run to the rock, rock was a-melting,

G
Run to the rock, rock was a-melting,

Am
Run to the rock, rock was a-melting,

   G   Am
All on that day.

3. Run to the sea, the sea was a-boiling,
Run to the sea, the sea was a-boiling,
Run to the sea, the sea was a-boiling,
All on that day.

4. Run to the moon, the moon was a-bleeding,
Run to the moon, the moon was a-bleeding,
Run to the moon, the moon was a-bleeding,
All on that day.

Now practice the alternating thumb roll with "Oh, Sinner Man." The pattern is shown below.

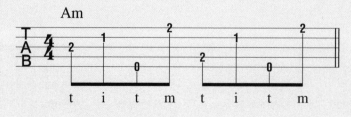

THE Em & D CHORDS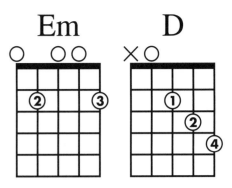
VIDEO 23

Study the fingering diagrams for the two new chords, Em and D. Memorize the letter names and the finger positions for each chord.

Practice both the melody and the new chords in this song. After you know the chord changes well, play the alternating thumb roll as you sing the melody.

THE DRUNKEN SAILOR

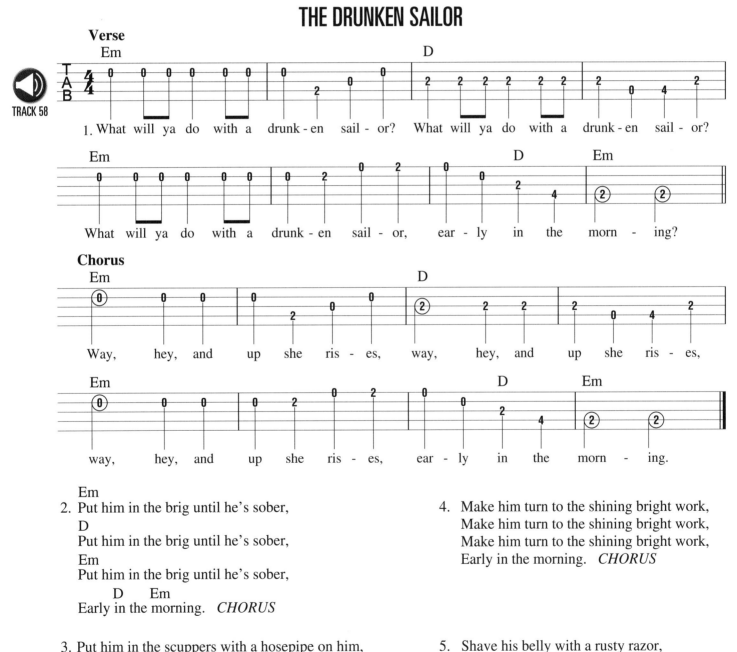

TRACK 58

Em
2. Put him in the brig until he's sober,
D
Put him in the brig until he's sober,
Em
Put him in the brig until he's sober,
      D   Em
Early in the morning. *CHORUS*

3. Put him in the scuppers with a hosepipe on him,
   Put him in the scuppers with a hosepipe on him,
   Put him in the scuppers with a hosepipe on him,
   Early in the morning. *CHORUS*

4. Make him turn to the shining bright work,
   Make him turn to the shining bright work,
   Make him turn to the shining bright work,
   Early in the morning. *CHORUS*

5. Shave his belly with a rusty razor,
   Shave his belly with a rusty razor,
   Shave his belly with a rusty razor,
   Early in the morning. *CHORUS*

Be sure to practice the alternating thumb roll with both of these songs.

THE CUCKOO

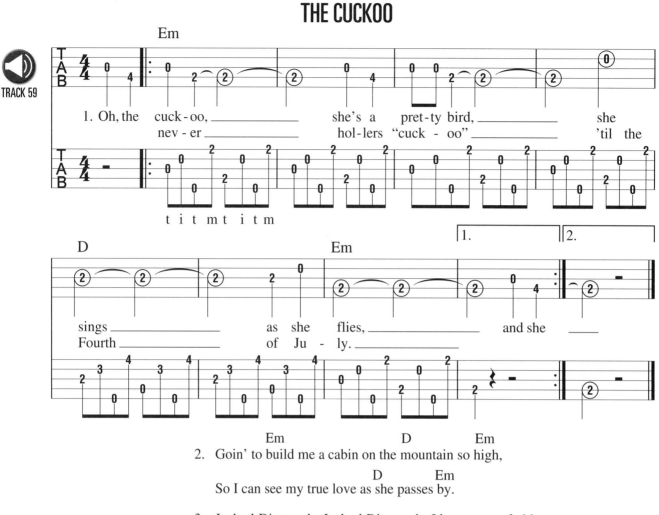

TRACK 59

1. Oh, the cuck-oo, _____ she's a pret-ty bird, _____ she
   nev-er _____ hol-lers "cuck - oo" _____ 'til the

t i t m t i t m

sings _____ as she flies, _____ and she
Fourth _____ of Ju - ly. _____

              Em   D   Em
2. Goin' to build me a cabin on the mountain so high,
                        D   Em
So I can see my true love as she passes by.

3. Jack o' Diamonds, Jack o' Diamonds, I know you of old.
You robbed my poor pockets of silver and gold.

4. I'm troubled, yes, I'm troubled, I'm troubled in my mind.
If this trouble don't kill me, I'll live a long time.

SHADY GROVE

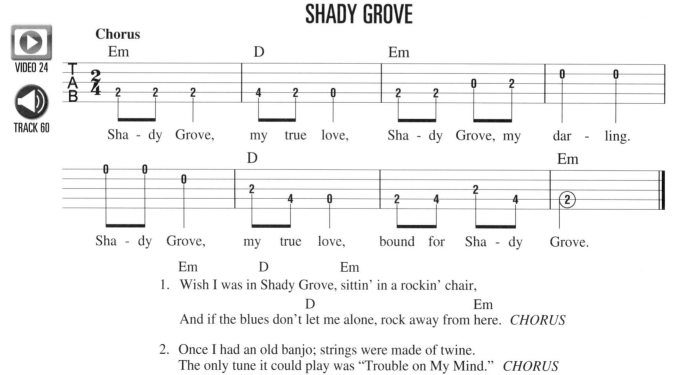

VIDEO 24

TRACK 60

Chorus

Sha - dy Grove, my true love, Sha - dy Grove, my dar - ling.

Sha - dy Grove, my true love, bound for Sha - dy Grove.

        Em   D   Em
1. Wish I was in Shady Grove, sittin' in a rockin' chair,
                     D   Em
And if the blues don't let me alone, rock away from here. *CHORUS*

2. Once I had an old banjo; strings were made of twine.
The only tune it could play was "Trouble on My Mind." *CHORUS*

THE FORWARD ROLL

The **forward roll** is based on the right-hand finger pattern t i m. Notice that this pattern moves across the strings from 5 to 1.

In "The Streets of Laredo," the forward roll begins with the index (i) finger. This song is in 3/4 time signature, which is three beats per measure. We will cover more 3/4 time later on in the book. For now, this three-beat pattern serves as a good introduction to the forward roll.

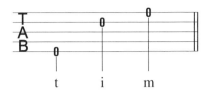

THE STREETS OF LAREDO

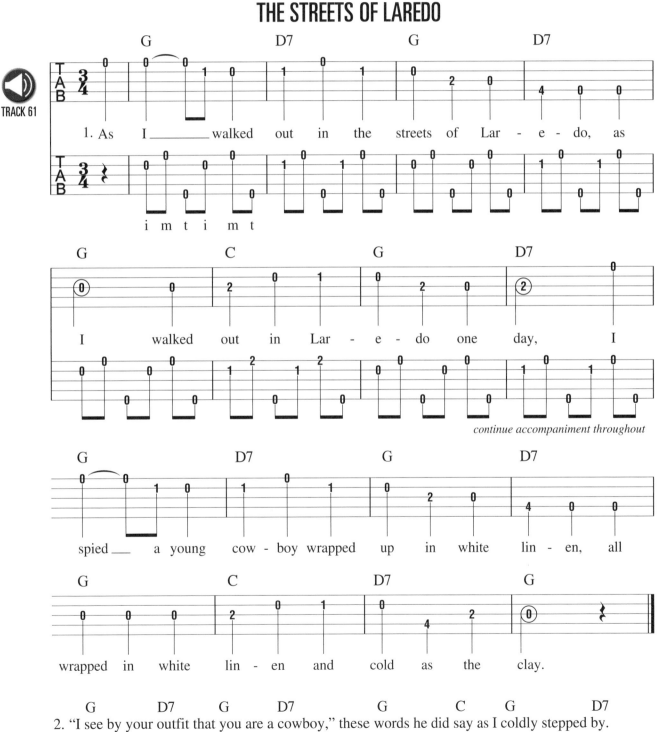

continue accompaniment throughout

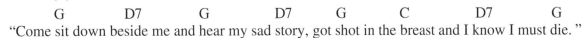

G   D7   G   D7   G   C   G   D7
2. "I see by your outfit that you are a cowboy," these words he did say as I coldly stepped by.

    G   D7   G   D7   G   C   D7   G
    "Come sit down beside me and hear my sad story, got shot in the breast and I know I must die."

THE BASIC FORWARD ROLL

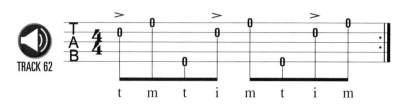

VIDEO 25

The common four-beat form of the forward roll uses the thumb in place of the index finger at the beginning of each measure. Watch the accents as you practice the basic forward roll.

When you can play the basic forward roll smoothly, play it as accompaniment to "This Little Light of Mine."

THIS LITTLE LIGHT OF MINE

FORWARD ROLL VARIATIONS

The accompaniment pattern to "Green Corn" uses this new variation of the forward roll:

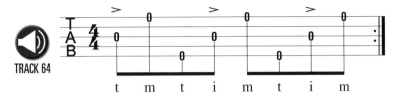

TRACK 64

When you feel comfortable with the index finger on string 3, play the accompaniment to "Green Corn."

GREEN CORN

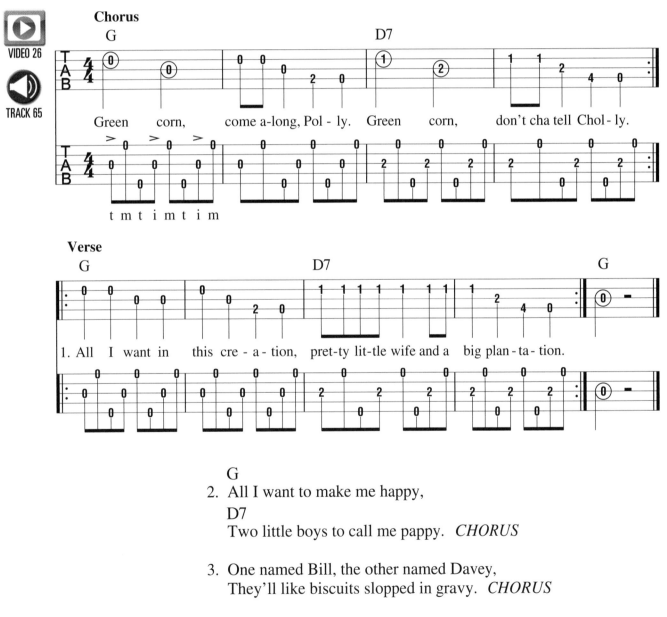

VIDEO 26

TRACK 65

Green corn, come a-long, Pol - ly. Green corn, don't cha tell Chol - ly.

t m t i m t i m

Verse

1. All I want in this cre - a - tion, pret-ty lit-tle wife and a big plan - ta - tion.

G
2. All I want to make me happy,
D7
Two little boys to call me pappy. *CHORUS*

3. One named Bill, the other named Davey,
They'll like biscuits slopped in gravy. *CHORUS*

4. All I need in this creation,
Three months work and nine vacation. *CHORUS*

The basic roll is usually altered so that melody notes can be added to the roll pattern. This alteration is done by moving the thumb or index finger to different strings to play the melody. The example below shows a new variation.

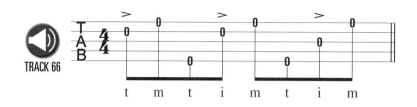

In the following song both the melody and the banjo arrangement are shown. In the banjo arrangement the melody notes are accented and should be played louder. Practice each part slowly and carefully. For the remainder of the audio with this book, the banjo handles the melody notes.

BOIL THEM CABBAGE DOWN

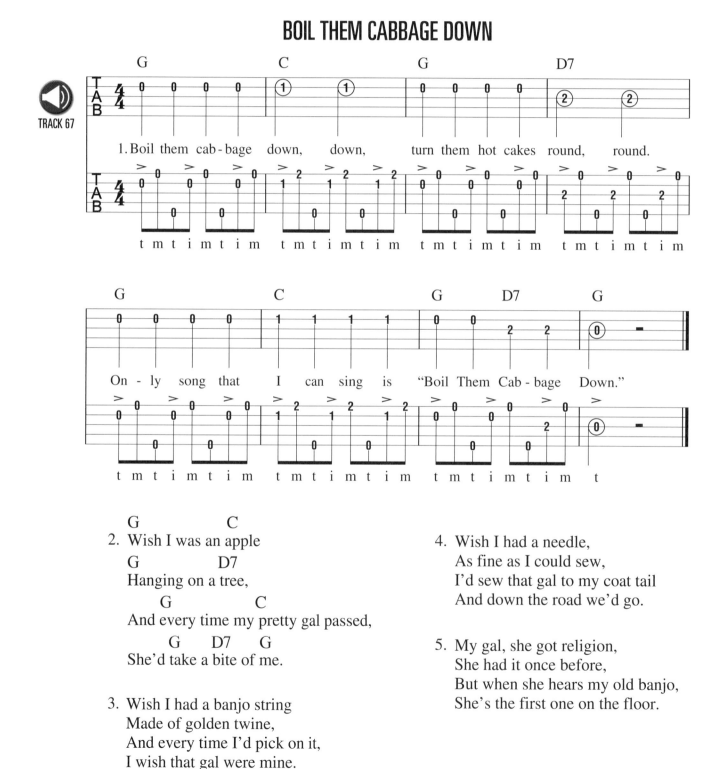

         G   C
2. Wish I was an apple
         G   D7
   Hanging on a tree,
          G   C
   And every time my pretty gal passed,
          G   D7   G
   She'd take a bite of me.

3. Wish I had a banjo string
   Made of golden twine,
   And every time I'd pick on it,
   I wish that gal were mine.

4. Wish I had a needle,
   As fine as I could sew,
   I'd sew that gal to my coat tail
   And down the road we'd go.

5. My gal, she got religion,
   She had it once before,
   But when she hears my old banjo,
   She's the first one on the floor.

THE FORWARD-BACKWARD ROLL

Another common roll in bluegrass banjo playing is the **forward-backward roll** (sometimes called a **reverse roll**). Practice the roll and each variation slowly and carefully. If you have difficulty, practice the smaller parts first.

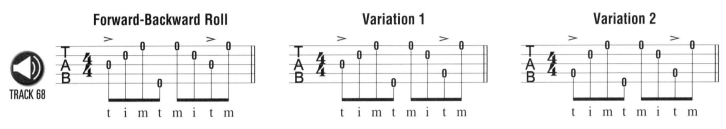

Now practice the melody, then the banjo arrangement of "Do Lord." After you have learned both parts, you should be able to play the banjo part as you sing the melody.

Notice that the roll pattern changes in measures 3, 10, and 11. This is the forward roll you have already learned and occurs when the melody moves to the second string. Be sure to look at the rolls before playing any new song so you will know where different rolls occur.

DO LORD

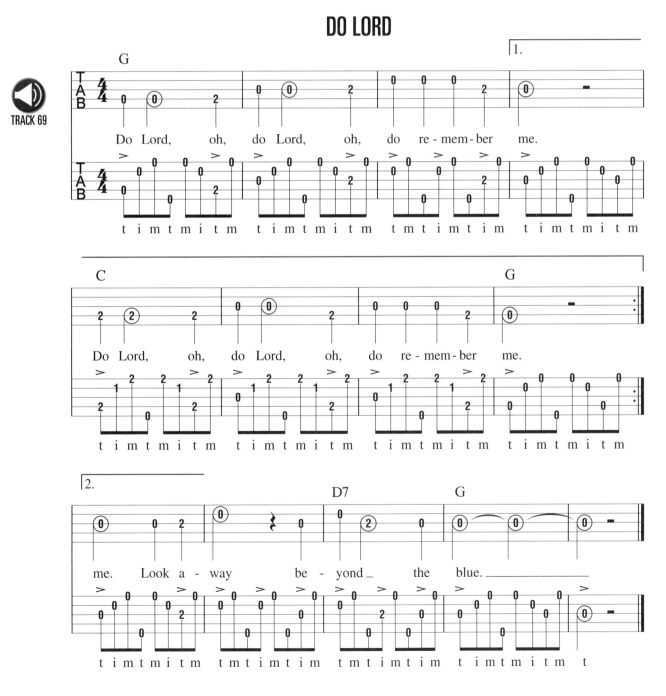

The next songs use all three types of rolls you have learned. Look at the banjo arrangement part and find each roll pattern before you play the song. If any are difficult for you to play, isolate them and practice them separately.

After you can play the arrangement part well and you know the melody, sing as you play the rolls.

HAND ME DOWN MY WALKING CANE

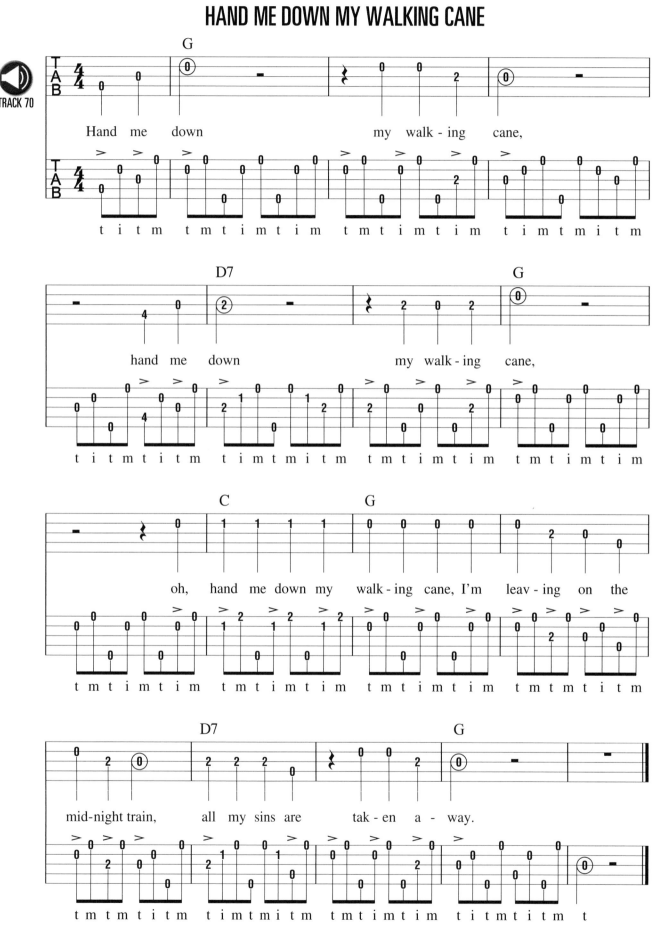

Practice the melody and the banjo arrangement carefully.

HARD, AIN'T IT HARD

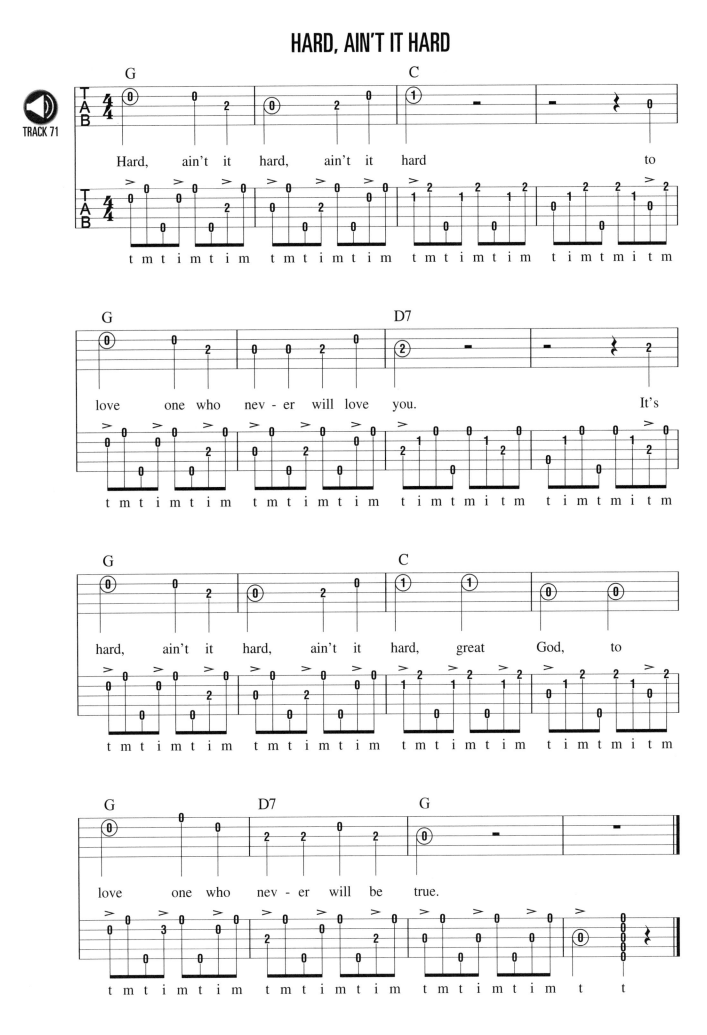

THE PINCH

When two or more strings are plucked at the same time, it is called a **pinch**. Bluegrass banjo players most often use the pinch on strings 1 and 5. Practice the following exercise several times combining the pinch and the melody notes of "Goodnight Ladies."

GOODNIGHT LADIES

Now try out the pinch in "The Old Grey Mare."

THE OLD GREY MARE

THE HAMMER-ON

VIDEO 27

Up to now, all the notes you played have been plucked or strummed by the right hand. Notes can also be added to a melody using three left-hand techniques.

The first of these left-hand techniques is called the **hammer-on**. Try the following examples of hammered-on notes in two steps. The letter "h" is used to indicate the hammer-on.

Step 1. Pluck the open string with the right hand.
Step 2. Strike the string, or "hammer" down with the tip of the left-hand finger indicated.

The finger must strike quickly near the fret to produce a clear sound. Listen to the demonstration of this technique on the recording. Practice each example until you can play them easily and smoothly.

TRACK 74

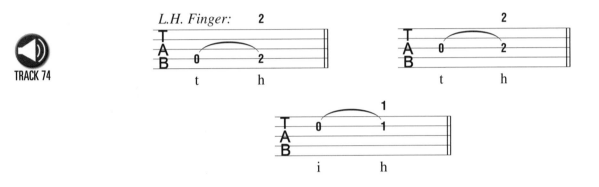

Practice each hammer-on exercise separately many times until mastered. Strike the hammer-on on the second half of the beat to produce two even eighth notes.

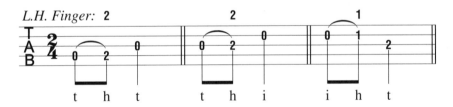

The hammer-on can be used as a pickup or introduction to a song, or within a roll. Practice the following example.

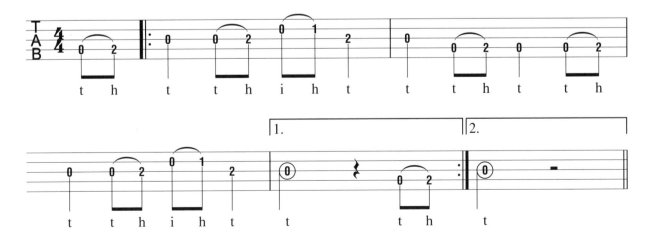

SIXTEENTH NOTES

When a note is hammered-on in a roll, the left-hand finger often falls between the two right-hand notes. The two notes of the hammer-on equal the time of one eighth note. When an eighth note is equally divided into two parts, each part is called a **sixteenth note**. Sixteenth notes look like this: ♬. Two sixteenth notes equal one eighth note.

Try each basic roll with a hammer-on added. Be sure to play each sixteenth note evenly. You'll be using the forward roll in "Old-Time Religion" in the following ways:

TRACK 75

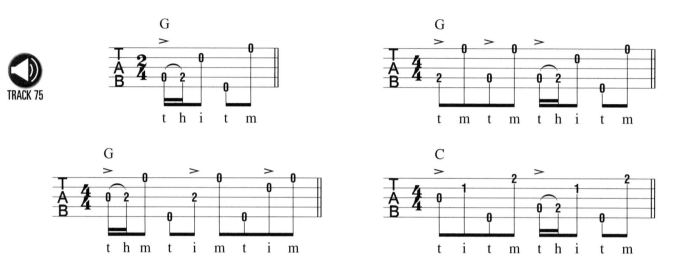

OLD-TIME RELIGION

TRACK 76

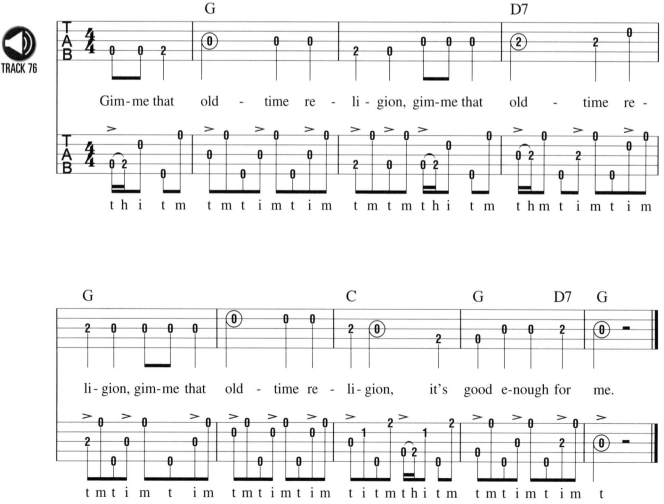

Here's another classic tune including hammer-ons and sixteenth notes.

SHE'LL BE COMIN' 'ROUND THE MOUNTAIN

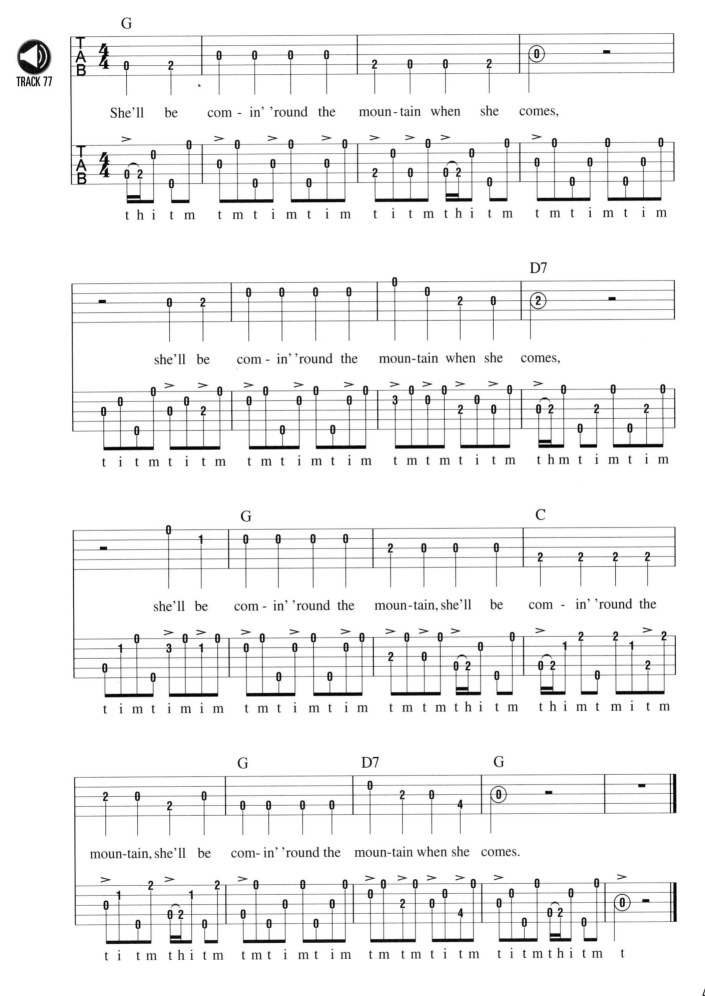

THE PULL-OFF

VIDEO 28

The second left-hand technique you should develop is the **pull-off**.

Now try the following examples of pull-off notes in two steps. The letter "p" is used to indicate the pull-off.

Step 1. Pluck the string with the right hand. Be sure you are using the correct left-hand finger and fret.

Step 2. Maintain pressure as you pull the left-hand finger toward the palm of the hand that is sounding the string.

Listen to the demonstration of this technique on the recording. Practice each example until you can play them easily and smoothly.

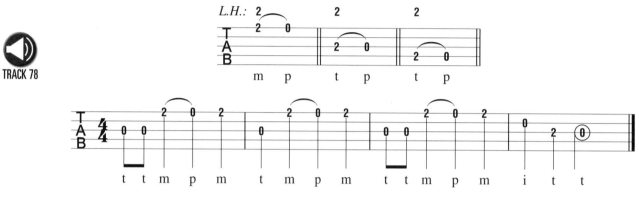

TRACK 78

Try each of the basic rolls with the pull-off added. Be sure to play each sixteenth note evenly.

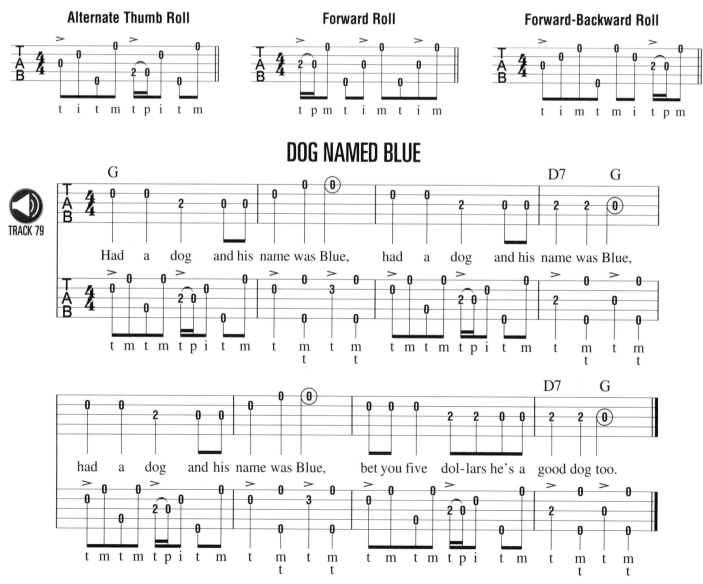

Alternate Thumb Roll   **Forward Roll**   **Forward-Backward Roll**

DOG NAMED BLUE

TRACK 79

Had a dog and his name was Blue, had a dog and his name was Blue,

had a dog and his name was Blue, bet you five dol-lars he's a good dog too.

46

THE SLIDE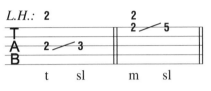
VIDEO 29

The **slide** is the third left-hand technique you will need.

Now try the following examples of slides in three steps. The slide is indicated by the letters "sl."

Step 1. Fret the string with the left-hand finger indicated.

Step 2. Pluck the string with the right-hand finger indicated.

Step 3. Maintain pressure as you move the left hand to the fret shown in the second part of the slide.

Listen to the demonstration of this technique on the recording. Practice each example until you can play them easily and smoothly.

TRACK 80

Try each of the basic rolls with the slide added. Be sure to play sixteenth notes evenly.

BOIL THEM CABBAGE DOWN

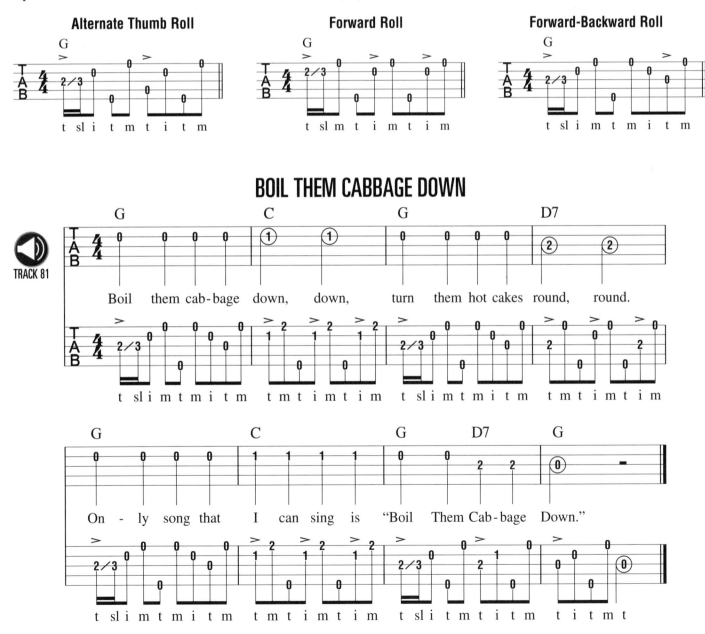

Combine all the techniques and rolls you have learned to play in "Cripple Creek"—a well-known bluegrass song. Be careful to play the first slide smoothly and evenly, and not too fast.

CRIPPLE CREEK

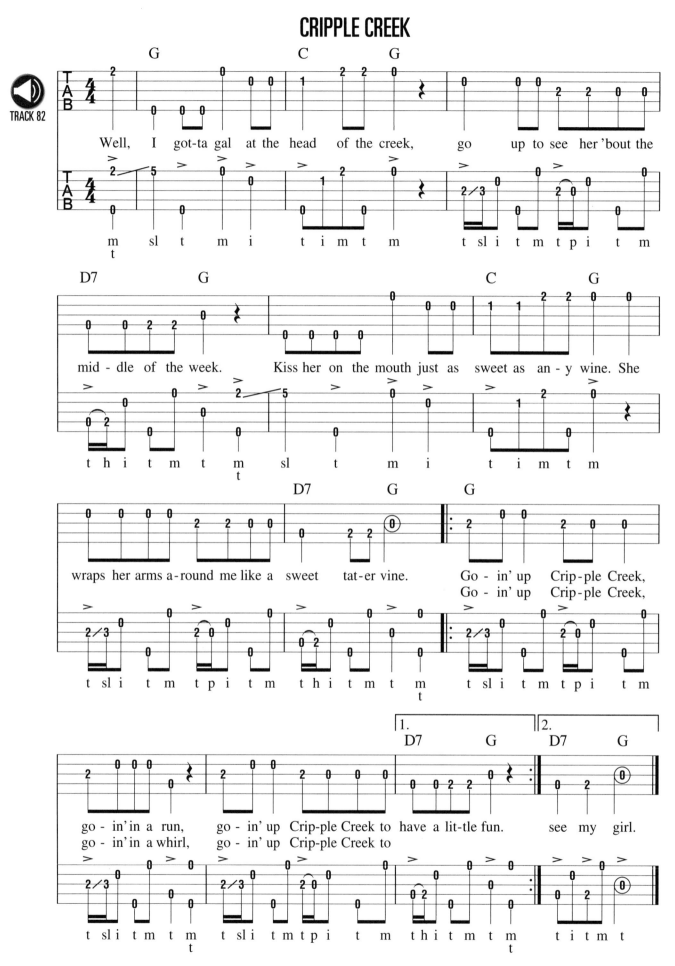

Here's another great tune to test out your bluegrass chops!

MY HOME'S ACROSS THE BLUE RIDGE MOUNTAINS

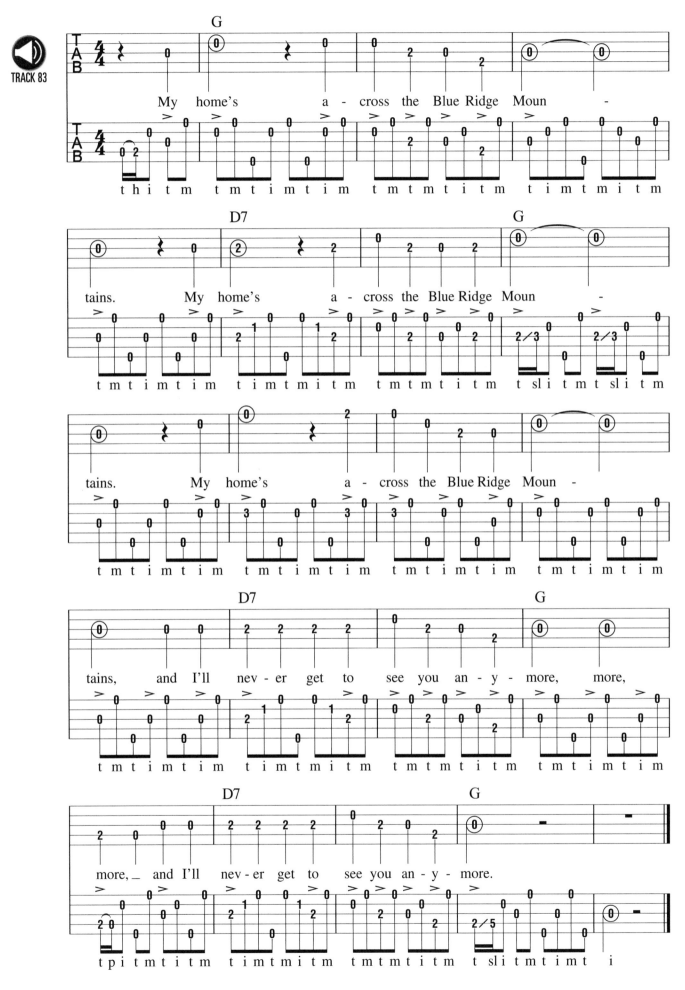

Practice the following variations in which the thumb and index finger move to different strings. After you can play them easily and accurately, use them in "Worried Man Blues."

TRACK 84

WORRIED MAN BLUES

TRACK 85

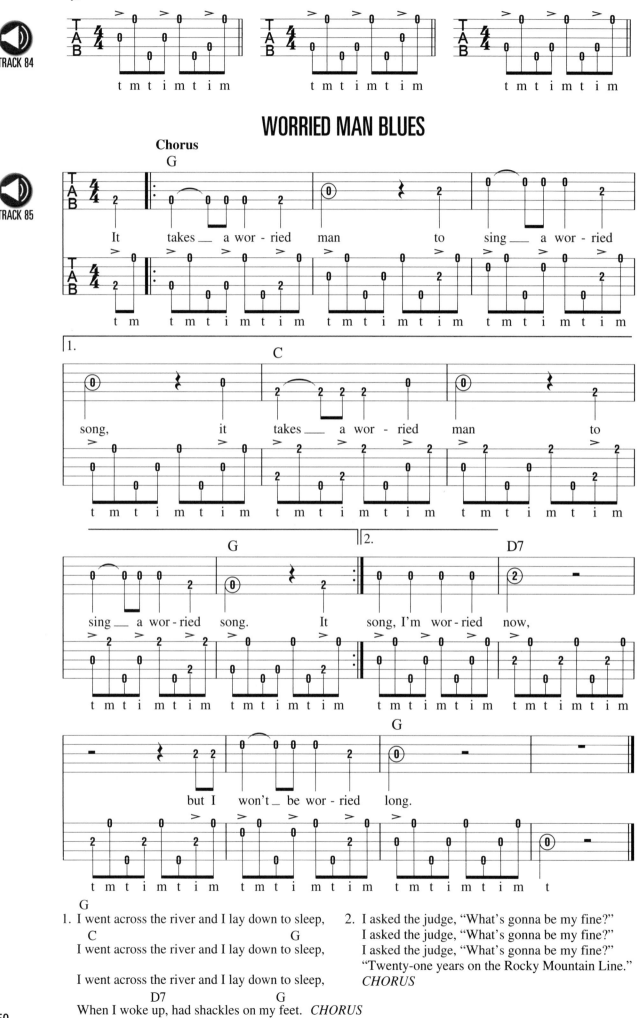

G
1. I went across the river and I lay down to sleep,
      C   G
   I went across the river and I lay down to sleep,

   I went across the river and I lay down to sleep,
                 D7   G
   When I woke up, had shackles on my feet. *CHORUS*

2. I asked the judge, "What's gonna be my fine?"
   I asked the judge, "What's gonna be my fine?"
   I asked the judge, "What's gonna be my fine?"
   "Twenty-one years on the Rocky Mountain Line."
   CHORUS

Practice each roll pattern before playing "Jesse James." Be sure to play slowly and accurately at first, then increase your speed.

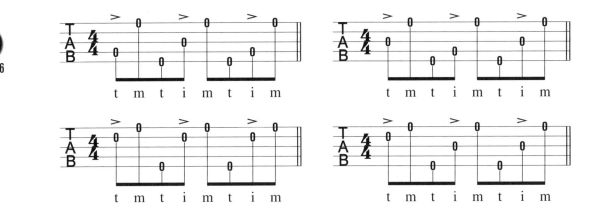

JESSE JAMES

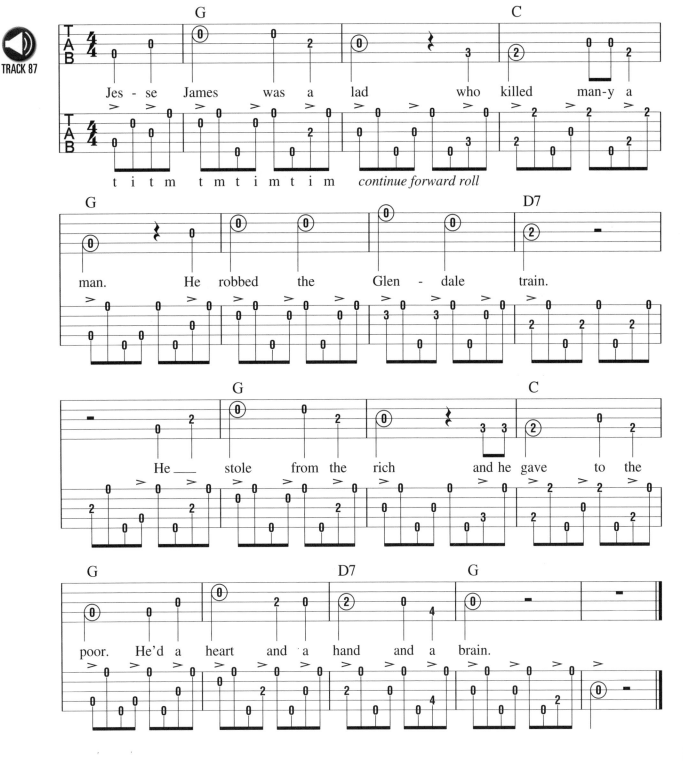

Play the melody to "Foggy Mountain Top" which appears on the top line of tablature until you are familiar with it. Then strum the chords as you sing the verses. After you are familiar with the melody and words, play the banjo arrangement that appears on the bottom line of tablature. The banjo part includes techniques that have been previously introduced.

FOGGY MOUNTAIN TOP

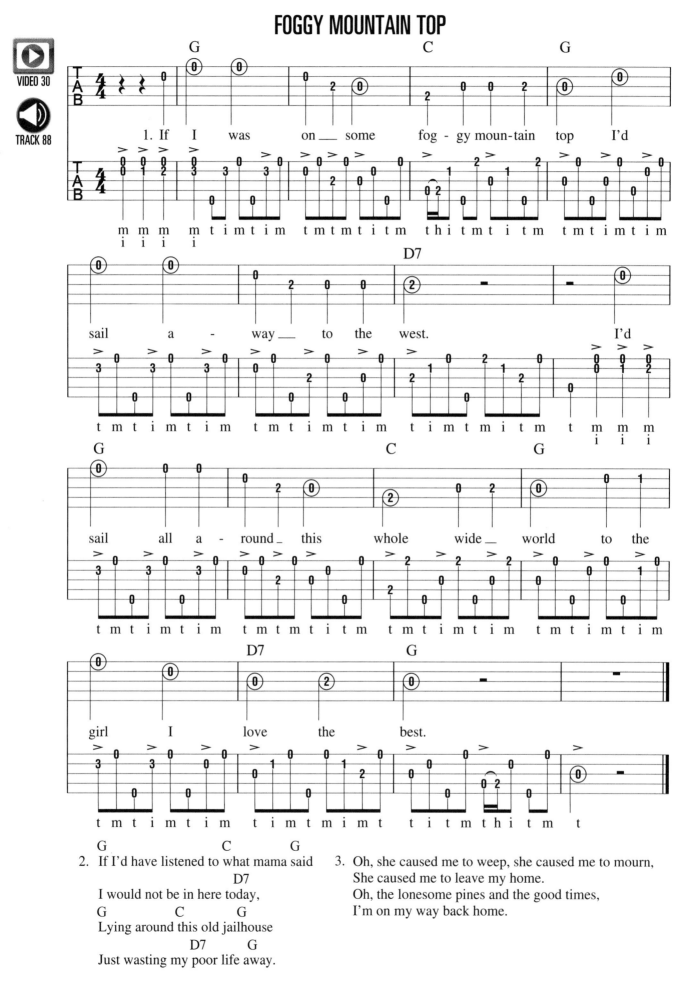

VIDEO 30

TRACK 88

2. If I'd have listened to what mama said
   I would not be in here today,
   Lying around this old jailhouse
   Just wasting my poor life away.

3. Oh, she caused me to weep, she caused me to mourn,
   She caused me to leave my home.
   Oh, the lonesome pines and the good times,
   I'm on my way back home.

Use the same procedure for "Little Birdie" that you used for "Foggy Mountain Top." Learn the melody first, then play the banjo arrangement.

LITTLE BIRDIE

TRACK 89

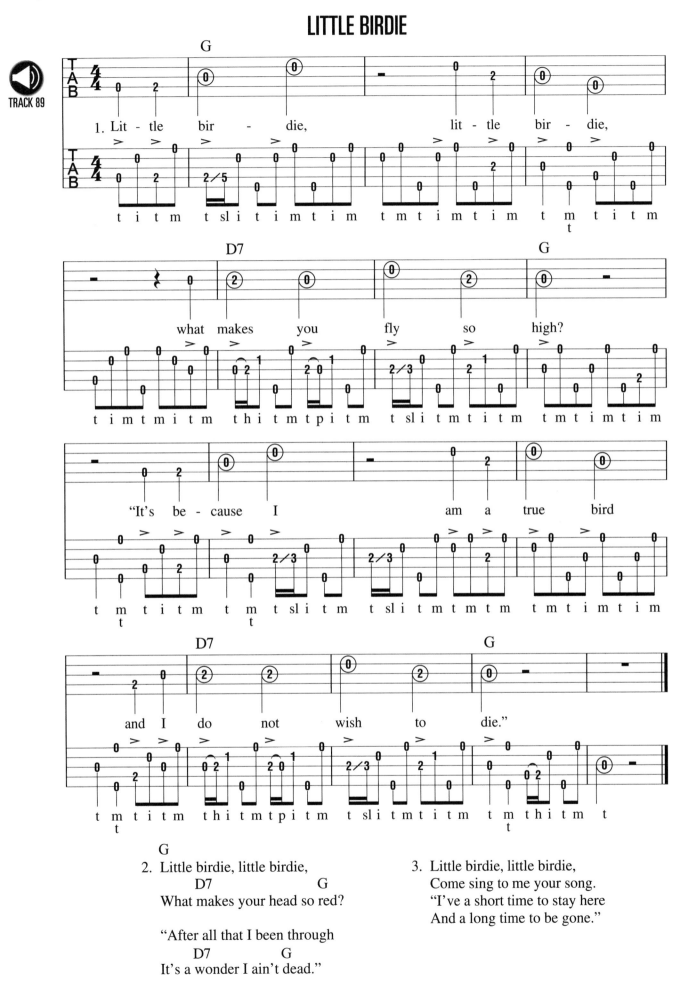

2. Little birdie, little birdie,
   What makes your head so red?

   "After all that I been through
   It's a wonder I ain't dead."

3. Little birdie, little birdie,
   Come sing to me your song.
   "I've a short time to stay here
   And a long time to be gone."

THE Dm, A & A7 CHORDS VIDEO 31

Study diagrams below for the finger position of the Dm, A, and A7 chords.

Strum strings 4 through 1 only when playing the Dm chord.

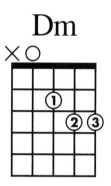

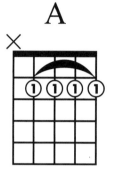

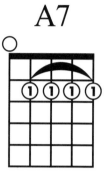

The A chord is played by placing the index finger across the strings at the second fret. This is called a **bar** or **barre** (pronounced the same). Check out the photos below to see the barre technique. Strum strings 4 through 1 only for the A chord. To play A7, finger the A chord, but strum *all five* strings.

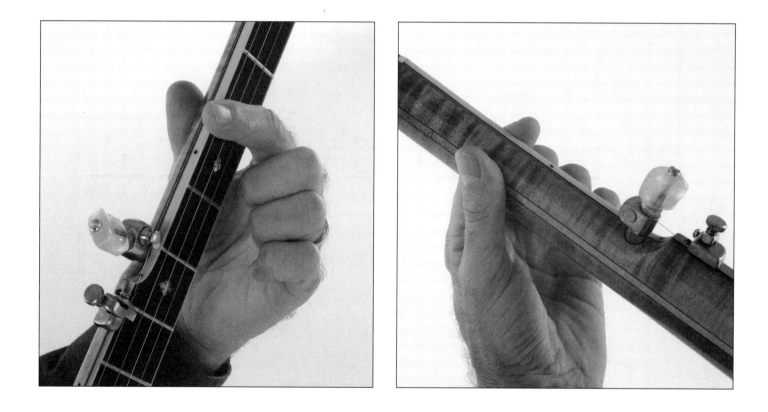

Play the following exercise to practice these new chords.

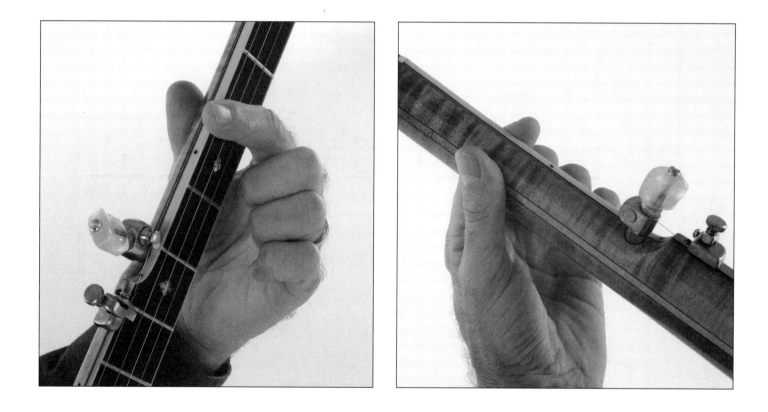

Strum and sing the new chords in this next song. Play one strum per beat.

WADE IN THE WATER

VIDEO 31 (cont.)

TRACK 90

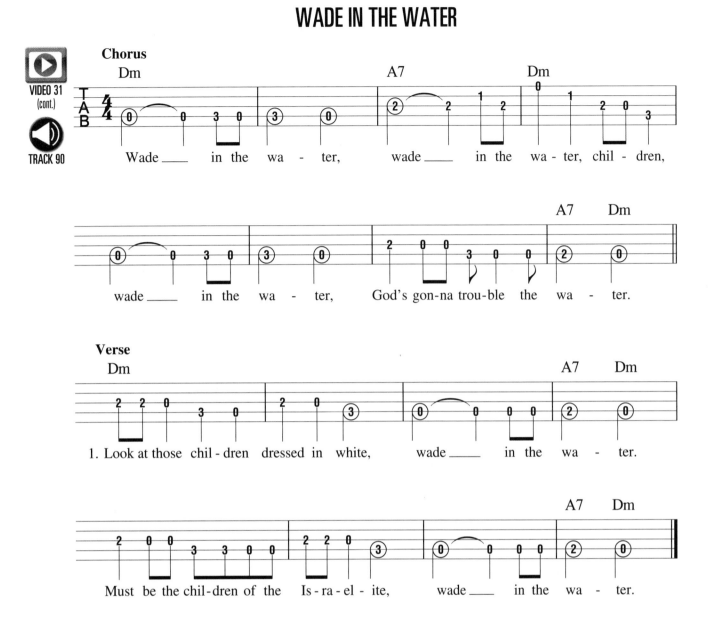

Chorus

Wade ___ in the wa - ter, wade ___ in the wa - ter, chil - dren,

wade ___ in the wa - ter, God's gon-na trou-ble the wa - ter.

Verse

1. Look at those chil - dren dressed in white, wade ___ in the wa - ter.

Must be the chil-dren of the Is - ra - el - ite, wade ___ in the wa - ter.

Dm   A7 Dm
2. Look at those children dressed in black, wade in the wa - ter,
                A7 Dm
  Must be the hypocrites turnin' back, wade in the wa - ter. *CHORUS*

3. Look at those children dressed in red, wade in the water,
  Must be the people that Moses led, wade in the water. *CHORUS*

3/4 TIME

3/4 time, also known as waltz time, has three beats per measure. A basic accompaniment pattern for songs in 3/4 time goes like this:

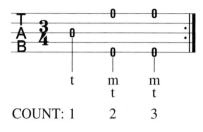

Play the chords to "Down in the Valley" using this new pattern.

DOWN IN THE VALLEY

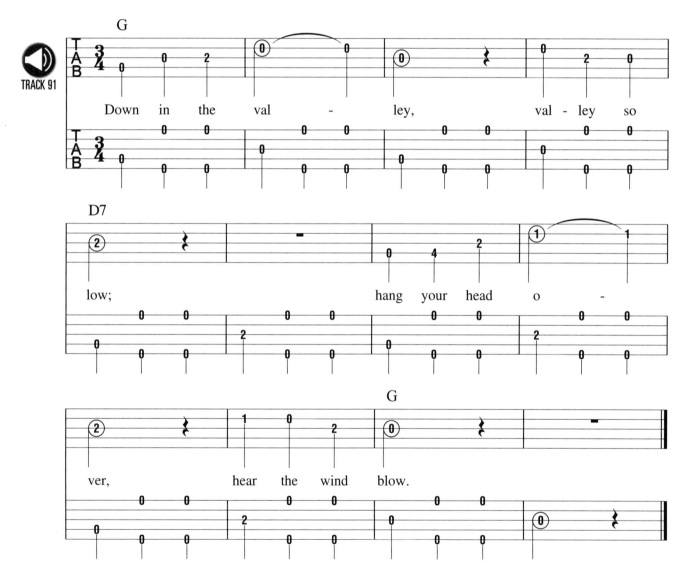

56

Once you've got the basic accompaniment for "Down in the Valley" under your fingers, try playing this arrangement that combines the melody with the basic 3/4 time pattern.

DOWN IN THE VALLEY

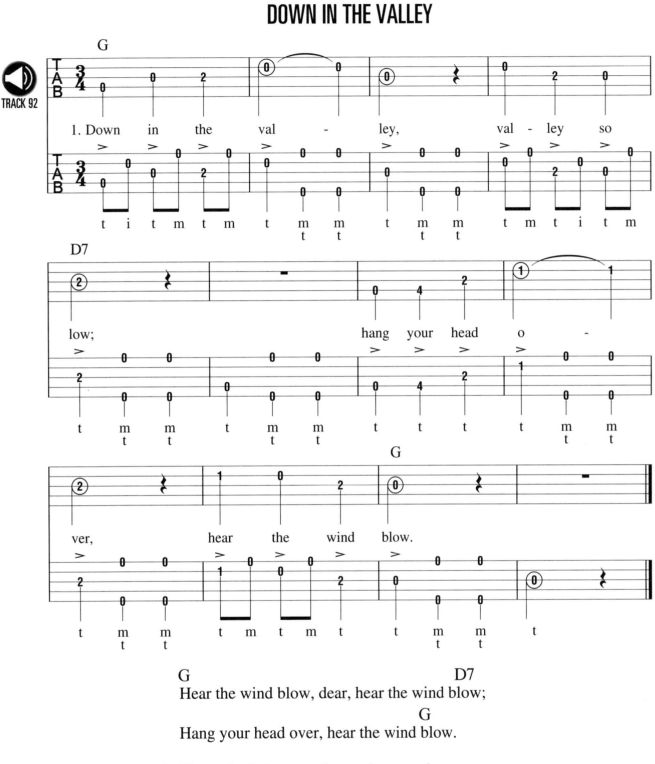

G
Hear the wind blow, dear, hear the wind blow;
                                        D7

Hear the wind blow, dear, hear the wind blow;
                                        G
Hang your head over, hear the wind blow.

2. If you don't love me, love who you please,
   But throw your arms 'round me, give my heart ease.
   Give my heart ease, love, give my heart ease,
   Throw your arms 'round me, give my heart ease.

Here are several more tunes in 3/4 to try out.

RYE WHISKEY

TRACK 93

Verse

1. If the o - cean was whis - key and I was a duck, I'd dive to the bot - tom and nev - er come

Chorus

up! Rye whis - key, rye whis - key, rye whis - key I cry! If you don't gim-me rye whis - key I sure - ly will die.

G

2. But the ocean ain't whiskey,

And I ain't no duck,

So I'll play Jack O'Diamonds
       C   G
And trust to my luck.

3. Let me eat when I'm hungry,
   And drink when I'm dry.
   If the hard times don't kill me
   I'll live 'til I die.

ALL THE GOOD TIMES

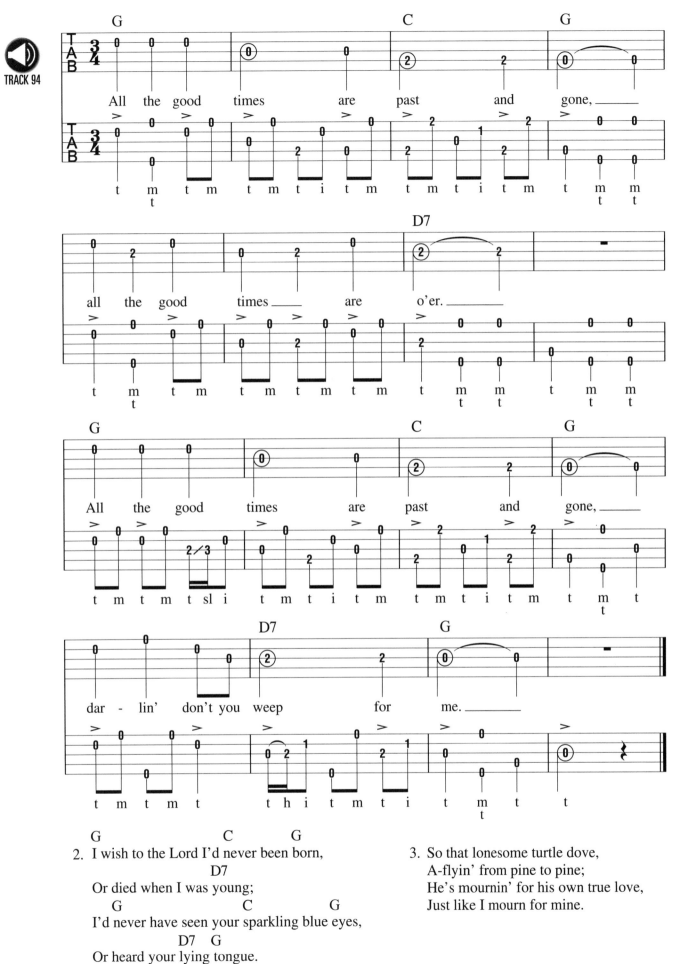

2. I wish to the Lord I'd never been born,
Or died when I was young;
I'd never have seen your sparkling blue eyes,
Or heard your lying tongue.

3. So that lonesome turtle dove,
A-flyin' from pine to pine;
He's mournin' for his own true love,
Just like I mourn for mine.

The banjo part for "Long Journey Home," shown on the next page, uses a new right-hand roll.

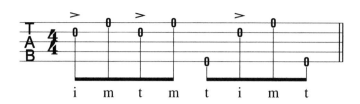

Notice that this roll begins with the index finger. Be sure to use the correct right-hand fingering as you practice this new roll.

A variation of this roll used in "Long Journey Home" looks like this:

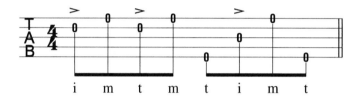

Play each of these new patterns, then try using them in this example.

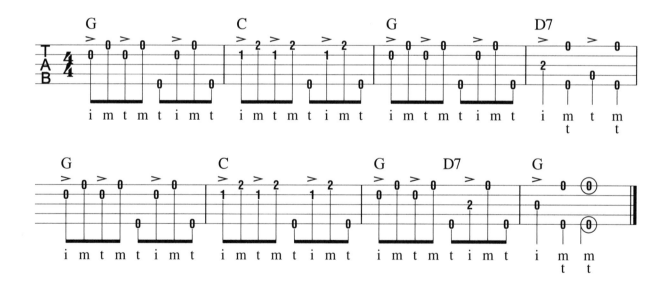

After you are familiar with the melody, play the banjo arrangement. Notice that the forward rolls in measures 4, 6, and 12 begin with the index finger of the right hand rather than the thumb.

LONG JOURNEY HOME

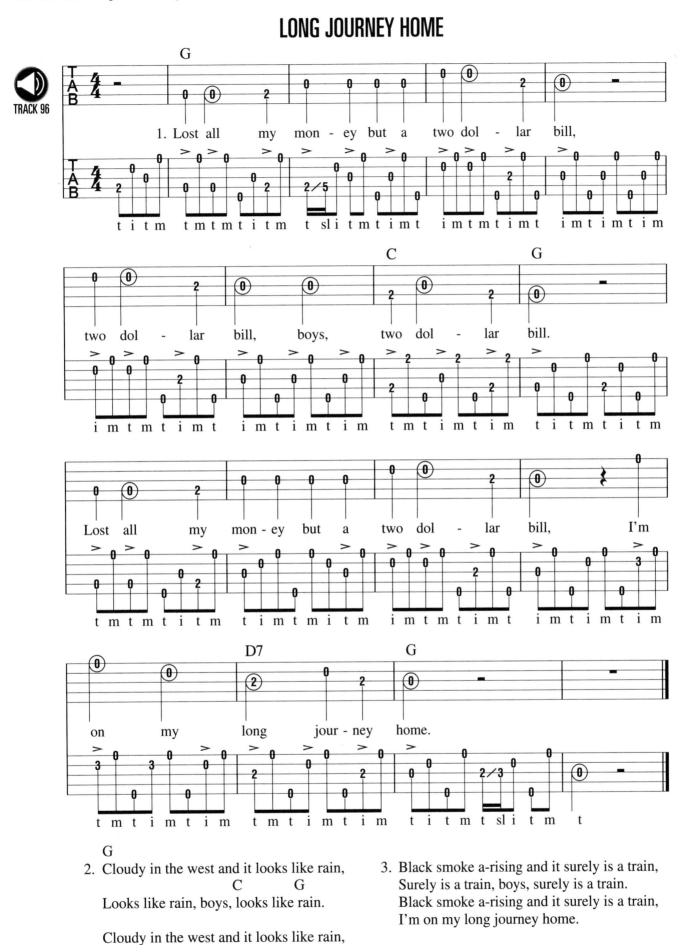

G

2. Cloudy in the west and it looks like rain,
   C   G
   Looks like rain, boys, looks like rain.

   Cloudy in the west and it looks like rain,
   D7   G
   I'm on my long journey home.

3. Black smoke a-rising and it surely is a train,
   Surely is a train, boys, surely is a train.
   Black smoke a-rising and it surely is a train,
   I'm on my long journey home.

This song is great for group singing. Learn the melody and words first, then play the banjo part.

ROLL IN MY SWEET BABY'S ARMS

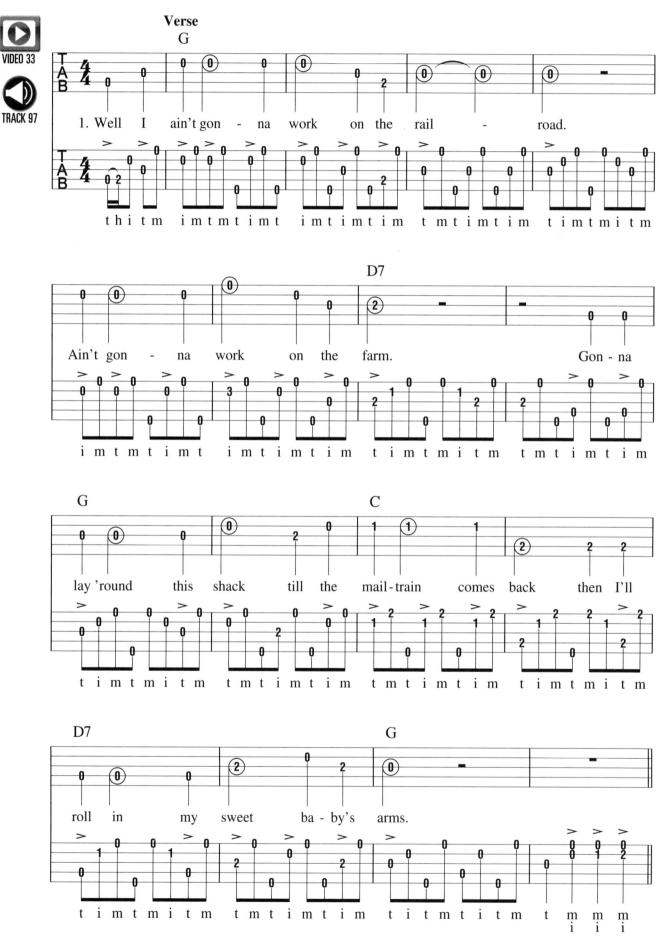

Chorus

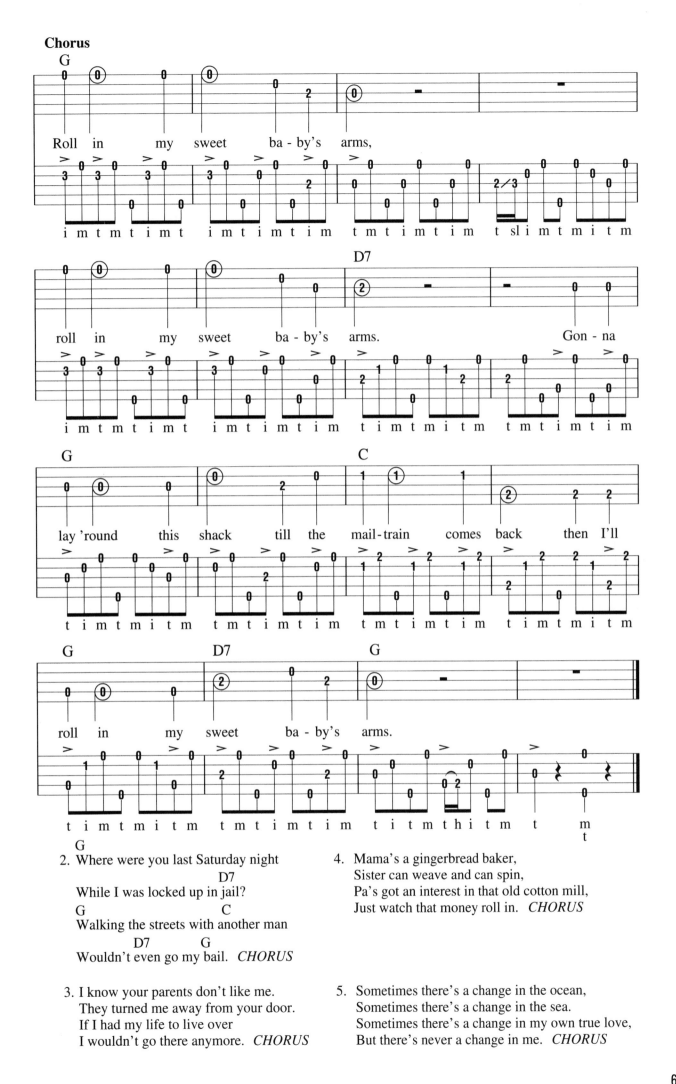

2. Where were you last Saturday night
   While I was locked up in jail?
   Walking the streets with another man
   Wouldn't even go my bail. *CHORUS*

3. I know your parents don't like me.
   They turned me away from your door.
   If I had my life to live over
   I wouldn't go there anymore. *CHORUS*

4. Mama's a gingerbread baker,
   Sister can weave and can spin,
   Pa's got an interest in that old cotton mill,
   Just watch that money roll in. *CHORUS*

5. Sometimes there's a change in the ocean,
   Sometimes there's a change in the sea.
   Sometimes there's a change in my own true love,
   But there's never a change in me. *CHORUS*

CHORD CHART

COMMON CHORDS FOR BANJO IN G TUNING

"X" indicates string is silent

"O" indicates string is part of chord

A
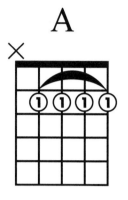

A7
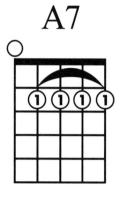

Am
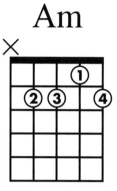

B7
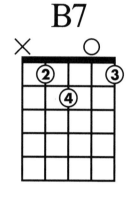

C
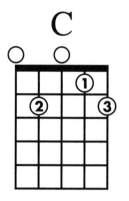

C7
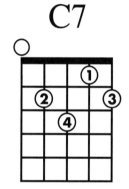

D
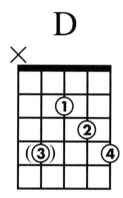

D7
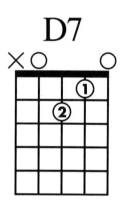

Dm
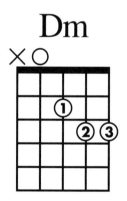

E
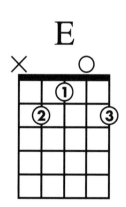

E7
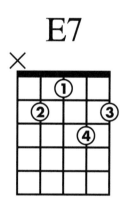

Em
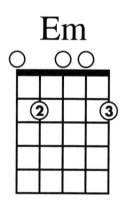

F
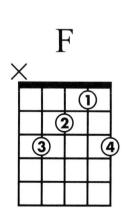

F7
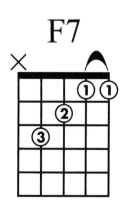

G
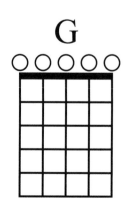

G7
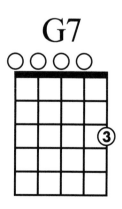